D1418525

ROSSINI

On the cover:
Gioachino Rossini (1792-1868)
Painting by Mayer (1820)

Facing page: bust of Gioachino Rossini
(Museum of La Scala Theater)

Text by:
Pierluigi Alverà
Marco Spada
Translated by:
Raymond Rosenthal

Published by Treves Publishing Co.,
a division of Elite Publishing Corporation
120 East 56th Street (Suite 1520)
New York, N.Y. 10022

Book designed by: Fenice 2000, s.r.l., Milano, Italy

Library of Congress Catalog Card No. 86-16168
ISBN 0-918367-11-5
Portraits of Greatness: Trade Mark Reg. No. 1,368,932

Printed and bound in Italy:
Officine Grafiche Sagdos, Milano, Italy - October 1986

Portraits of greatness

ROSSINI

by
Pierluigi Alverà

**TREVES
PUBLISHING
COMPANY**

INTRODUCTION TO ROSSINI

Today we will tell you the thoughts and memories of Gioachino Rossini, the blithe spirit. And also the sublime and sarcastic thoughts which he dictated, and those collected by his contemporaries and by modern students of his music and personality.

Rossini the man and Rossini the composer are still in search of their authenticity. During the past century his very music was subjected to such manhandling that a critical revision of his entire work, which is still in progress, became necessary.

We have tried to get to the truth about Rossini, a truth in tune with the musical gallop that over the span of his youth carried him from 18th century-inspired farce to romantic and epical drama and then for many long years stranded him in an exhausted, mysterious silence.

The one person who did not make our task any easier is Rossini himself. Older people sometimes repeat the same anecdote again and again without variation. On the contrary, Rossini supplied two or more versions of the most salient events of his life. In this, too, his originality is greater than ours.

This brief study has to some extent helped us in our own attempt at understanding the enigma of Rossini the man. One thing is clear: such a man could only have been born in Italy, although in his time he was a true citizen of Europe. His life is proof that, thanks to the universal language of music, he felt at home in every capital and every small European village.

Commemorative fan with portrait of Gioachino Rossini framed by the titles and characters of his operas (La Scala's Theatrical Museum, Milan).

Throughout the 18th century and after, the "journey to Italy" was a categorical imperative for every young man on the other side of the Alps who aspired to complete culture. His journey had Rome as its most enlightening stage and its most prolonged sojourn. The city displayed its grandeurs of art and history and its political complications to the gaze of these cultivated tourists. (Alongside: the Quirinale, residence of the popes; above: a painting by Pannini with details of 18th century Rome; opposite page, right: a 19th century Pontifical banner.)

AS SEEN BY STENDHAL

Stendhal (below on left) made his first "journey to Italy" in the entourage of Napoleon's armies in 1796. For the writer it was love at first sight (the country, the music, the women...) and it had a vividly illuminating effect on all his subsequent literary production. Among his many books in which Italy and its people played the part either of protagonists or background figures, his biography of the maestro from Pesaro is brilliant and full of verve. Yet, strangely enough, the two great men never met nor did they have any sort of contact.

"Buonasera, mio signore, buonasera, buonasera..."

And one more time: *buonasera*, good evening, ladies and gentlemen. When calling Rossini a "blithe spirit," someone was perhaps carried away by tradition or, more precisely, by Rossini's most illustrious biographer, the writer Henry Beyle, better known by his *nom de plume* Stendhal, who, instead of studying Rossini's life and character, was the first to invest him in legend. And yet, even before giving a colorful description of his subject, Stendhal set down a description of Italy that, almost two hundred years later, no Italian can altogether refute.

«The Italian political situation,» Stendhal says, «is far from enviable. But from Raphael to Canova, from Pergolesi to Rossini, all men of genius destined to enchant the world with the fine arts, are born in the country where one must

love. The very faults of the strange governments that afflict Italy are at the service of the fine arts and love. The Papal Government does not exact total submission from its subjects. It is content if they pay their taxes and go to Mass. And so it permits the circulation of many dangers in society. Everyone is free to do whatever comes into his head in order to secure his particular pleasure, whether it be poisoning his rival or worshipping his mistress. The government, abhorred and despised since time immemorial, does not mould opinion or have any influence. It goes through society, but it is not inside society».

Stendhal knew Italy very well, but he could not claim that he knew Rossini. When *Il Barbiere di Siviglia* (The Barber of Seville) had already conquered all of Europe, he was not yet a successful writer and perhaps that is why he never knocked at the door of the maestro who would have been only too glad to welcome him.

IN QUEST OF GREAT MUSIC

Between L'Italiana in Algeri *(here in an amusing picture from the La Scala production of 1984 with Ponnelle's direction, scenery and costumes)* Il Barbiere di Siviglia *and* Guillaume Tell *(below, in a 19th century lithograph) unfolds the course of activity dedicated by Rossini to the musical theater. The Maestro crowns and* concludes *an ancient formula which has its roots in the* Commedia dell'arte, *whereas in* Barbiere *he offers us his definitive word on opera buffa, in* Guillaume Tell *he opens the path for the new romantic melodrama which will be followed by Verdi in Italy and by grand opera in France.*

A child of the arts, Rossini had the best education an artist can hope for. This gave him the strength, if only for a few hours a day, and for a limited number of years, to overcome his puny propensity for work – a constant trait of his character – and above all it helped him endure what he considered the decadence and mediocrity of a certain Italian theatrical milieu.

After the glorious days of Vivaldi and Pergolesi, great music had migrated north of the Alps. Italian composers, seduced by a taste for opera, lost all contact with instrumental and symphonic music which, although it too was born in Italy, was recreated by the genius of Hadyn, Mozart, and Beethoven. When he was only twelve, Rossini tried to resume with his sonatinas for strings the dialogue with European musical trends.

But quite soon his gay spirit had to fall in line with the tendencies of the time, and so he turned to the theater. The Rossini scholars of today say that he tried to improve a taste that was as insatiable for new operas as it was contemptuous of any substantial innovation and that with his help music regained control over the vanity and capricious antics of the singers.

By transforming comic opera into a comedy of character, and by infusing serious opera with a vitality and humanity unknown until then, Rossini added a new dimension to Italian melodrama. Straddling two centuries, as we mentioned before, Rossini closes the cycle of comic opera with *L'Italiana in Algeri* and opens the cycle of national melodrama with *Guillaume Tell*. After him, in the space of a few years, Bellini, Donizetti and Verdi appeared.

View of Pesaro, Gioachino Rossini's native city, from the San Bartolo Hill in a 19th century painting (opposite page below); above left, again Pesaro, a detail of Piazza Grande in a picture from "Illustrazione Popolare" of 1892.

11

FIRST ECCENTRICITIES

Rossini was born in Pesaro, a pretty town on the Adriatic coast in Central Italy which at the time was under Papal rule. The day was the 29th of February in the leap year of 1792, and his coming into the world on that day of all days was his first eccentricity. His second eccentricity, six or seven years later, was to write his name – Gioacchino – whith one "c" instead of two, that is, Gioachino, unlike all those with the same name always did and always will write it. His father, Giuseppe Rossini, had the not altogether substantiated reputation of being the impoverished scion of a patrician family. Due to his boisterous, vivacious personality, he was nicknamed *Vivazza*. He played the horn and the trumpet at Bologna's Teatro Civico. Europe was just on the point of being disrupted by many years of war, and in 1797, when the French occupied Pesaro, Giuseppe Rossini, having become "Citizen Vivazza", conducted the municipal band beneath the Tree of Liberty. At the age of six, Gioachino was accepted in Pesaro's revolutionary armed forces in the capacity of *listaro* or player of the metal triangle in the percussion section which is called the *lista*. But actually he was the band's mascot. His mother, Anna Guidarini, came from a poor family with many beautiful daughters. She knew nothing about music or singing, but her naturally fine voice and her extraordinary memory enabled her to learn any role very quickly. Watching and listening to her was one of the boy's greatest joys during his poor childhood.

While the parents travelled from town to town, earning the meager wages offered by theaters in those days, the boy was entrusted to his maternal grandmother. At school he had the reputation of being lazy, disobedient, and quick to use his fists. Near the end of his life, Rossini received a letter from a childhood friend who, after thanking him for an autographed photograph, wrote: «I still have on my neck the scar left by a stone that Your Most Illustrious Excellency threw at me when Your Excellency was a torment rather than a delight to the entire world». In 1802 Anna was engaged in Trieste to sing the

Thomas Memorial Library
Wednesday, 5-APR-00 5:02p
7601007439000 Hampton, Deborah A.

Due: 03-May-00, Wednesday
  Item: 760191000152019S 921 ROSSINI
  Rossini

Hageman 926-9080 Thomas 926-7696

Rossini was born in Pesaro in a house (opposite page, above) located in the street that now bears his name. He was the son of parents who were both musicians; his father, Giuseppe (below, his presumed portrait) was a trumpet player who came from Lugo, his mother a fine singer. The city has formed a cult around its most illustrious citizen. His name has been given to the Music Conservatory (opposite page below, the conservatory's marble hall) and the theater, of which on this page to left we see the facade; below, the auditorium, and at the bottom the theater's curtain called "Of the Muses".

13

In the 19th century opera was by far the most popular form of entertainment. «This kind of art is one of the most splendid inventions that man has ever made», John Evelyn already wrote in his Diary in 1654. It attained its highest peaks during Rossini's century. The theater was its shrine, concretely embodied in the sophisticated form of tiers with boxes (below: the Apollo theater in Rome). These small cells were the observatory from which to watch the show and a show-case to display oneself to the city's elite, exhibit gowns, complicated coiffures, and jewels, like those of the lovely ladies depicted at the La Scala and printed here below.

role of *seconda donna* in a by now forgotten opera. The *prima donna* was Giuseppina Grassini, a contralto of great beauty, endowed with a magnificent voice and the mistress of many powerful figures, among whom – so rumor had it – was Napoleon Bonaparte himself. Gioachino was then ten years old, and he went to Trieste with his parents. His mother's success was so great that half the audience began to show its preference for her. Disturbed by some expressions of disapproval mingled with the applause, Giuseppina Grassini fainted – or pretended to faint – and the performance had to be halted. At the next performance Anna was regaled with an avalanche of catcalls by Grassini's claque, and she in turn pretended to be taken ill. Quicker than his father and quicker even than the stagehands, Gioachino dashed out on stage to assist her, all the while staring challengingly at the audience. The performance then continued without further incident.

The high spirits shown by the boy on this and other occasions convinced the parents that it might perhaps be more prudent for him to study composition instead of singing, a career for which he seemed destined by his beautiful voice. Gioachino took his first lesson in counterpoint in Bologna under the guidance of the excellent Father Stanislao Mattei. A year later he realized that his mother's voice was beginning to deteriorate and that the time had come to think of helping his parents.

At the age of thirteen, while playing the viola at the Sinigaglia Theater not far from Pesaro, Gioachino tried to correct the opera's leading lady. She was a beautiful young woman, Adelaide Carpano, the protégée of the impresario Marchese Cavalli, and she had a reasonably good voice. However, in a cadenza after her big aria she kept going off, singing intolerably off-key. The boy politely told her that she should make an effort to keep in harmony with the orchestra, and she seemed to agree. But in the next performance, Adelaide Carpano was again carried away by her fanciful inspiration, with disastrous results. Gioachino burst out laughing

From his earliest years Rossini had to deal with the singers' whims and headstrong behavior – an old bane of his profession already stigmatized by Benedetto Marcello in his caustic attack The Theater à la Mode. *The good qualities and weaknesses of these favorites of the public are* highlighted very neatly in this 18th century painting of the Bolognese school (La Scala's Theatrical Museum) which portrays the singer Teresa Lanti seated at a spinet, an instrument similar to that represented on the left and preserved in Bologna.

and the entire audience with him. Infuriated, the prima donna reported his uncouth behavior to the impresario. That austere gentleman told the boy that while he had the courage to make fun of a first-class artist, he, on the other hand, had the power to throw him into jail. Gioachino refused to be intimidated and frankly explained why he did what he did.

In school in Bologna Rossini was the despair of his teachers, because he was in fact an autodidact. In his old age he told Wagner: «I sedulously copied the scores of *Die Schöpfung*, (The Creation), *Le Nozze di Figaro* (The Marriage of Figaro), and *Die Zauberflöte* (The Magic Flute). Sometimes I transcribed only the vocal line. Then, on a separate sheet of paper, I wrote an orchestral accompaniment of my own invention, and, finally, I compared it to the original. This method of working served me better than all the courses in the Conservatory».

At times the boy neglected his studies to earn a living working as an accompanist on the harpsichord, singing in church, and composing sacred music. His lack of patience brought about his expulsion from school.

AL NOBIL UOMO IL SIG. CONTE E CAV. PIETRO GHERARDI

ESCAPED PERILS

Inexhaustible hot-bed of singers, Italy was also the country of those "emasculated singers" who attracted the satire of Giuseppe Parini. Endowed with steady voices with an unmistakable timbre, very highly paid and pampered by the public, some of them reached the heights of the most unbridled star mentality such as Carlo Broschi, called the Rogue, who is portrayed below. Nature had bestowed a beautiful voice on Rossini as a boy, but the fate of a male soprano was avoided, luckily for him and for us, because of his mother's determined opposition.

At the age of thirteen, Gioachino already admired the lovely ladies who came to hear him sing in Bologna's churches and drawing rooms. One of his mother's brothers, Francesco Guidarini, a barber by trade, tried to convince Gioachino's parents that it would be advisable to use artificial means so that the boy's beautiful voice lasted longer. Since they were poor and Gioachino had shown a talent for music, this could have become a good source of income for the whole family. The majority of *castrati*, and especially those who undertook a theatrical career, lived in opulence. "Citizen Vivazza" was ready to follow this advice and, if it weren't for his mother's adamant opposition, Rossini would have become part of that corporation or, more precisely, that de-corporation, as he put it when an adult. A year after his last soprano concert, Gioachino heard a young Spanish artist sing in Bologna. Her name was Isabella Colbran and during those years she was in the service of His Catholic Majesty, the King of Spain. A celestial voice, the contemporary chroniclers declared. And a great beauty, whom he was able to admire only from a distance, without imagining for a moment the role she was to play in his art and life. But new clouds quickly gathered over Rossini's young head. The Napoleonic wars continued to rage in Europe. Fortunately, when he was about to be called up for military service, his success had arrived. Gioachino knew that he could count on the friendship of Prince Eugene Beauharnais, the son of the deposed Empress Josephine and in those years Viceroy of Milan. In 1812, when an entire generation was dying at the Beresina, he appealed to the Prince, who was then in Russia with Napoleon, and was given permission to devote himself to more peaceful activities. «Conscription came out ahead», he said later, «because I would have made a very poor soldier».

The "Parnasus of the singers", etching at the end of the 18th century with medals of the most famous virtuosi of the period.

SUCCESS

In August 1810, Rossini met in Bologna Giovanni Morandi and Rosa Morolli, his parents' artistic colleagues, who had witnessed the stormy clash with Adelaide Carpano and the Marchese Cavalli in Sinigaglia. They were on their way to Venice, where that same impresario was preparing a season of four one-act comic operas for the Teatro San Moisé.

Before long, Cavalli ran into trouble. Three of the four farces were not well received by the public and a fifth, promised by a German composer, never arrived. Morandi spoke to the impresario about the impertinent boy – whom he in fact remembered with pleasure – and was authorized to ask him if he wanted to try his luck in Venice.

The beat of Rossini's heart outraced his step as he crossed the theater's threshold. He was handed a libretto entitled *La Cambiale di Matrimonio* (Marriage by Promissory Note). He wrote

the score in a few days and Cavalli took the risk of staging the opera. During rehearsals, some of the singers found the orchestration too heavy and the vocal line not always agreeable. More than just a theater's season was at stake. Because his family was anxiously awaiting the forty *scudi* he had promised to send, Gioachino hid in his small lodgings and wept in despair. Morandi consoled him by helping him re-copy the score, incorporating the requested corrections. Tempers were calmed, and *Cambiale*, which opened on the 3rd of November, 1810, had a run of thirteen performances. Cavalli had kept his promise. Perhaps forty *scudi* was not very much. But never before had Rossini seen so many.

In June 1812, the twenty-year-old maestro was offered one hundred and twenty *scudi* for an opera to be performed at La Scala – three times the amount paid for *La Cambiale di Matrimonio*. Maria Marcolini and Massimo Galli, who

Here below and on opposite page: three moments from La Pietra del Paragone in the La Scala production (1981-82), with the direction of Eduardo De Filippo and scenery and costumes by Mario Chiari. In this gay and tender opera, Rossini tells the story of a count who wants to be loved for his soul, not for his money. He pretends to be a Turkish merchant who has come to seal the Count's property (that is, his own) rapping out a series of imperious orders expressed with the maccaronic word "Sigillara!" «This word» Stendhal declared, «made such an impression on Milan, on this people born for *the beautiful, that it brought about a change in the opera's name. If you speak of* Pietra del Paragone *in Lombardy nobody understands you; you've got to say* Sigillara*!». Opposite page, above: Marietta Marcolini and Filippo Galli, famous interpreters of* L'Italiana in Algeri.

had sung his music before, contributed to his being engaged by Italy's foremost theater. The opera's libretto, *La Pietra del Paragone*, was an effervescent, burlesque farce which Rossini found most congenial. It was also a pretext to echo the theme, so dear to Mozart, of making fun of home-grown seraglios.

La Pietra del Paragone had a run of fifty-three performances in a single season at La Scala. Later, there were even more fortunate Rossini scores. In the late 19th century, in his novel "Piccolo Mondo Antico" (The Small Old World), the Italian novelist Antonio Fogazzaro slightly changed the lines of the famous Mississippi aria:

*Ombretta sdegnosa del Mississipí
non far la ritrosa ma baciami qui!*

(Oh, uppity little shadow of the Missipipi
Don't be so coy but give us a kiss.)

After its first tremendous success, *La Pietra* was not heard from again until its rediscovery in recent years.

Perhaps Stendhal is right when he says that musical taste is always renewed, at almost constant, fixed intervals.

La Pietra del Paragone was followed by nine operas in fifteen months. Rossini was caught between the demands of the impresarios on one side and those of the singers on the other. But he wrote the overtures for himself, to atone for his facile theatrical successes.

After *La Pietra*'s success at La Scala, an aristocratic Milanese beauty stole Gioachino away from the opera's main singer and made him a guest in her Brianza villa. Captivated by the amiable lady, and with her seated at the piano beside him, he wrote many new arias. However, she caught him at the piano with an aristocratic lady from Bologna. He sang a comic aria in their honor and then left them both in the lurch.

As for Rossini's comic arias, Riccardo Bacchelli says: «The repetition and the rhythmic-melodic distortion of words and phrases creates a kind of obsessive comic tone that we will find, far from music, in another master of rhythm and crescendo, Charlie Chaplin».

TRAVELLING THROUGH ITALY

Between 1810 and 1816 Rossini visited Italy's main cities. The first two weeks are devoted to attempts to improve the librettos submitted by the impresarios. Sometimes acts of the same libretto were handed to him at three different times and he had to compose the music without knowing the narrative, or even the conclusion. Then he had to worry about the singers, whose inadequacies made him sacrifice his own ideas. About twenty days before the *première*, Rossini sits down to compose surrounded by 'friends'. When at last he is alone, beautiful motifs come to him. «Composing is nothing», he says. «The real drudgery are the rehearsals. It's enough to call up your own cat-calls». The singers execute music which the Maestro re-composes and changes as they watch. Sometimes grotesque rows explode!

Finally, the great evening arrives. Rossini sits down at the harpsichord. At the end of the overture there is thunderous applause or resounding boos and catcalls. After each aria a moment of perfect silence is followed by an infernal din. After the third performance Gioachino collects his one hundred *zecchini*, then he climbs in the stagecoach to start the same adventure all over again in another city. En route, he never fails to have his little joke at his travel companion's expense – at times he pretends he is an enemy of Rossini's and parodies his most beautiful arias.

VENETIAN CATCALLS AND TRIUMPHS

In 1813, the Maestro made two long sojourns in Venice. At the end of January *Il Signor Bruschino* opened at the Teatro San Moisé. On the 12th of February, *Tancredi* opened at La Fenice, and on the 22nd of May came the turn of *L'Italiana in Algeri* at the Teatro San Benedetto.

The start of the season was stormy. With *Il Signor Bruschino*, the audience, vexed by a long delay, decided that the repeated tapping of the second violins' bows against the metal lamps which illuminated the score was too much of an eccentricity. Further but unfair protest was elicited by the brief motif, in a comic key, of a funeral march. There have been many versions of this opera's failure, which later was re-evaluated.

Tancredi's libretto was based on a tragedy by Voltaire. Performed the following year in all European countries and even in the remote Americas, *Tancredi* was Rossini's first successful opera. But in the enchanting frame offered by the Teatro La Fenice, Rossini had no way of knowing this. His ears still buzzed with the boos which the Venetians had bestowed on *Il Signor Bruschino* two weeks before, although in a different theater. As if that were not enough, the prima donna Madame Malanotte refused to sing her great aria, the wonderful "Di tanti palpiti" (So many heart throbs). A delicate motif which he perhaps had already heard somewhere else came to Rossini's rescue. The new aria was nicknamed "the aria of the rice" because it took Rossini less time to compose it than it took his cook to prepare a dish of rice. But after the second performance the "palpiti" or "throbbing" aria was restored, and in no time it was being sung by half of Italy.

In his poem "Don Juan", Lord Byron humorously alluded to the success of *Tancredi* and other Rossini operas in England:

«… the long evening of duets and trios!
The admirations and the speculations,
The "Mamma mia's" and the "Amor Mio's"!
The "Tanti palpiti's" on such occasions,
The "Lasciamo's" and the quavering "Addio's"»

On the page opposite, above: a scene is being mounted for Tancredi at the Rossini Opera Festival at Pesaro, 1982; at the center "A remote place on the outskirts of the city", a stage setting by Sanquirico also for Tancredi, 1829; below: the La Fenice Theater in Venice, where

Tancredi was first produced, before the fire that destroyed the theater. On this page, L'Italiana in Algeri at the Metropolitan Opera House in New York in December 1985; on the left: the singers being applauded; on the right: the soprano who sang the main part, Marilyn Horne.

1815 AND AN "ITALIAN MARSEILLAISE"

The comic, sensual and vaguely patriotic tones of *L'Italiana in Algeri* aroused great enthusiasm from the very start. On opening night the audience particularly applauded Marietta Marcolini, the magnificent prima donna. On the second night, Rossini received tremendous ovations while poems of praise fluttered down on him from all sides. Referring to the libretto, Gioachino said: «I thought that after hearing the opera, the Venetians would think I was crazy, but they turned out to be even crazier».

The theme of Italian military prowess, awakened by the Napoleonic epic, which three months earlier had resounded in *Tancredi*, appeared again in the finale of the new, successful comedy (with two brief and not particularly wonderful lines repeated frantically amid trumpet blasts and rejoicing crowds:

"... how much Italian valor counts... in battle we shall see..."

Then the schooner sailed away, right under the noses of the inevitable Turks, and gone was also the comic opera's last laugh.

Twenty years of tragic wars were coming to an end. But they did not affect Rossini until almost the last day. It took another Gioachino or Joaquin, Joaquin Murat, Napoleon's brother-in-law and for six years the King of Naples, who involved him in a risky adventure. Murat, in the struggle against Austria, took over the command of the few men who had not yet decided to lay down their arms. One of his rare initial successes consisted in occupying on April 5th, 1815, the town of Rimini, on the Adriatic, close to Pesaro and not far from Bologna, where he proclaimed Italy's independence.

There was an uprising in Bologna and Rossini was soon found to compose the Hymn of Independence. On April 15th he conducted it with Murat present.

The next day the Austrians recaptured Bologna. The hymn's music and words, which during its one-day existence was called "the Italian Marseillaise", vanished forever. Rossini's name was put on the list of subversives, but he had no serious trouble from the Austrian police.

Domenico Barbaja (above), before he became the "prince of impresarios", had the concession to manage the gambling tables in La Scala's lobby. Having become quite rich, he set about organizing operatic shows at the San Carlo in Naples, La Scala and in Vienna. His mistress was Isabella Colbran (alongside), famous Spanish contralto, who later became Rossini's wife and the interpreter of almost all of his operas (portraits at La Scala's Theatrical Museum).

On opposite page: a scene designed by A. Sanquirico for Elisabetta Regina d'Inghilterra, *1828.*

DOMENICO BARBAJA
AND ISABELLA COLBRAN

While Lombardy and the Venetian regions fell under Austrian domination, and while Rome and Bologna returned under Papal rule, after eight years of exile in Sicily Ferdinand IV made a triumphant return to Naples in May 1815, almost at the same time that Gioachino arrived in that Kingdom of the Sun.

In those years Naples was one of the most industrious, happy cities in Italy and on the theatrical plan it could boast of European supremacy. Besides the Royal Teatro San Carlo, perhaps the most beautiful and certainly the largest theater in the world, there were the Teatro Mercadante, the Teatro Nuovo, and, on and off, the Teatro San Carlino and the Teatro Fiorentini.

In that environment – and to all practical purposes its boss – existed a personage whose memory is still alive today, a legend in the Italian operatic world: the impresario Domenico Barbaja. He was of humble origin and after having run the gambling tables in La Scala's foyer, transferred to Naples when he was just over thirty and there learned to move with assurance in aristocratic and court circles. When the Teatro San Carlo was destroyed by fire in the winter of 1816, he had it rebuilt in less than a year. Barbaja had the reputation of being a gourmet and of having invented a drink composed of milk and chocolate with a sprinkle of ground coffee, which to this day is called the *barbagliata*.

Sovereign of that theatrical empire was a woman, more precisely, a prima donna, whom Stendhal described – and nobody dared contradict him on this point – as follows: «An imposing beauty, with features that are well delineated and superb on the stage, a magnificent figure, flashing "Circassian" eyes, a forest of raven hair and, above all, an instinct for tragedy. Her appearance on stage, with a diadem on her head, conquers and imposes absolute respect, even on people who have just left her in the foyer». She was the same beauty whom Gioachino had admired from a distance in his early youth in Bologna – her name was Isabella Colbran.

Rumor had it that Colbran and Barbaja were lovers. The lucky impresario needed only one more thing to consider himself completely happy: a composer to replace the late Cimarosa, and he felt he had found him in Rossini.

In seven years Barbaja put on as many as ten of Rossini's operas, among them *Elisabetta, Regina d'Inghilterra* (Elisabeth, Queen of England), *Otello, Mosé in Egitto* (Moses in Egypt), *La Donna del Lago* (The Lady of the Lake) and *Maometto II*, all composed for Colbran's admirable voice.

Quite a number of people suspected that Rossini had stolen Barbaja's mistress. We will say only that seven years later when Gioachino and Isabella got married, Barbaja bestowed his blessings.

Rossini's first Neapolitan opera was *Elisabetta*. English subjects were fashionable in those years, after England had finally won the war. The opera opened on October 4th, 1815, on the Crown Prince's birthday. The sovereigns and the prince attended the performance, which had the most flattering success. Soon the innate distrust for a composer who came "from the North" vanished.

THE FUNERAL OF DUKE CESARINI

Here below: a commemorative postcard of the Barbiere di Siviglia, *from a drawing by R. Paoletti, 1900 (Bertarelli Collection, Milan).*

His ties with Barbaja did not prevent Rossini from accepting commissions in other Italian cities. During those years, the impresario of Teatro di Torre Argentina in Rome was the Duke Francesco Sforza Cesarini. He offered Gioachino four hundred *scudi*, a third of the amount earned by the tenor Garcia for the same season, to compose an opera. The libretto was to be the impresario's choice, and the score was to be delivered within a month, with the composer on hand to assist the singers. The choice fell on *Il Barbiere di Siviglia*, which had already been set to music by many with mediocrity and exquisitely by Paisiello. It was certainly not with the idea of slighting the great Apulian composer that the young Maestro had decided to tackle a subject that the older man had developed so masterfully, and this was amply pointed out in the program. These precautions, however, did not prevent Paisiello's followers from lying in wait for the new opera, with feelings that were less than friendly.

We have a direct account of the *Barbiere's* opening night al Teatro Argentina from the mezzo-soprano Gertrude Righetti Giorgi, a Bolognese childhood friend of Gioachino's who, together with a splendid voice, possessed a rare intelligence and culture and who that evening was the opera's female protagonist:

«Rossini sat down at the harpsichord decked out in very peculiar looking tails adorned with gold buttons, and that produced the first laugh. With ill-advised condescension, he had agreed to Garcia's singing at the start under Rosina's window some Spanish arias of his own, and that was the beginning of the fiasco. In trepidation, I climbed onto the balcony to say: "Go on, my dear, do go on." The Romans, disappointed because those words were not followed by an amorous and pleasing aria, burst into boos and catcalls. Figaro's cavatina met with silence. Finally, I made my entrance, no longer at the window but on the stage. My aria, the aria of the "viper" (now called "Una voce poco fa") gave rise to a prolonged ovation. We thought the opera had been saved, but it wasn't. Envy, now enraged,

resorted to all its artfulness. We reached the stupendous finale of the first act amid laughter, screams and boos. Rossini made an applauding gesture at the singers, and the audience took it for a provocation. From the top-most balcony came shouts: "This is D.C.'s funeral!" A not very charitable allusion to Duke Cesarini's recent demise. But some people thought (in 1816) that the D.C., addressed to Rossini, meant "Don", followed by a word that does not bear repeating. During the second act, things got even worse. Gioachino left the theater with great dignity. Filled with anguish because of what had happened, I went to his house to console him. But he had no need for my consoling words for he was sound asleep.

«The next day the Maestro cut out Garcia's Spanish arias and replaced the opera's prelude with the overture to *Aureliano in Palmira*, which has since been known as the *Barbiere*'s overture. However, he did not feel up to sitting down at the harpsichord and pretended that he wasn't feeling well. The Romans decided that they might as well listen to the opera attentively in order to arrive at a fair verdict, and then the plaudits were general. Afterwards the imaginary invalid was complimented on the excellence of his work.

When the *Barbiere* toured Europe the philosopher Hegel wrote: «I've seen the *Barbiere* for the second time, and I'm afraid my taste must be depraved because this Figaro seems to me much more appealing than Mozart's».

First page of the contract between the Torre Argentina Theater in Rome and Gioachino Rossini for a comic opera, December 26, 1815. The result will be Il Barbiere di Siviglia. *Pressed for time, libretto and music were written with extraordinary speed, so that the opera could be presented on February 16, 1816.*

On the left: three of Palanti's costumes for La Scala's production of Barbiere *in 1905. On right: Gertrude Righetti Giorgi, the opera's first Rosina.*

THE TRAGEDY, THE FAIRY TALE AND A FABULOUS DISCOVERY

But by now, at the age of twenty-four, the Maestro was no longer satisfied to simply smile. He felt he could achieve new and more ample expressive dimensions in serious opera. Colbran's extraordinary vocal qualities, her imposing presence and her temperament, were incentives to search for inspiration in dramatic works. The Marchese Berio di Salsa, a personality of solid and vast culture, came to Gioachino's aid. We owe a lively description of his Neapolitan salon to that intelligent British traveler, Lady Morgan:

«The saloons of the Marchese Berio present another aspect of society equally favorable to the impressions previously received of Neapolitan intellect and education. In Rome a *conversazione* is an assembly where nobody converses, as in Paris a *boudoir* is a place "où l'on ne boude pas!" The *conversazione* of the Palazzo Berio, on the contrary, is a congregation of elegant and refined spirits, where everybody converses and converses well; and best (if not most) the master of the house».

At this house one met the finest artists of the period, from Canova to Rossini, and, as Lady Morgan continues, «While *Duchesse* and *Principesse*, with titles as romantic as that which induced Horace Walpole to write his delightful romance of "Otranto", filled up the ranks of literature and talent – Rossini presided at the piano-forte, accompanying alternately himself, the poet Rossetti in his impromptus, or Isabella Colbran, the prima donna of San Carlo, in some of her favorite arias from his own Mosé. Rossini, at the piano-forte, is almost as fine an actor as he is a composer. All this was very delightul and very rare!...».

And Berio wrote the libretto for *Otello*. Despite his culture and his charm he proved to be a very inept dramatist. Byron indignantly expressed his opinion in these terms: «They have been crucifying *Othello* into an opera (*Otello*, by Rossini): the music is good, but lugubrious; but as for the words, all the real scenes with Iago cut out, and the greatest nonsense inserted; the handkerchief turned into a billet-doux and the first singer

Giovanni Battista Rubini (left), the most highly regarded tenor of his period, here shown in Otello, *one of the ten operas written by Rossini for the Neapolitan theaters. Below: "Garden in Othello's house", a stage setting by Sanquirico, 1830. Bottom of page: Julia Hamari and*

Francisco Araiza in Cenerentola *at La Scala (1981-82). Also* Cenerentola, *first produced in Rome on January 25, 1817, was composed with dizzying speed. The story goes that Rossini was still looking for a subject to put to music the day before Christmas.*

would not black his face, for some exquisite reasons assigned in the preface». Despite all this *Otello* was quite successful at the Teatro del Fondo in Naples. Then it toured Europe, acquiring a lasting fame.

At the end of 1816, Gioachino went to Rome to compose an opera commissioned by the impresario Cartoni, who had him as a guest in his house.

«Cartoni, Rossini and I», the librettist Jacopo Ferretti said many years later, «had difficulties with the censors, who demand so many changes and of so many different kinds that it became impossible to do any of the subjects we proposed. After a tempestuous nocturnal meeting with the ecclesiastical censor, I accompanied Rossini back to his lodging. Tired of coming up with ideas, and half asleep, I yawned and mumbled: "Cinderella".

«Rossini, who had stretched out on his bed as if to improve his concentration, leaped to his feet and said:

«"Would you have the courage to write a Cinderella for me?"

«"How about you, would you have the courage to set it to music?"

«"When can you give me an outline?"

«"If I can stay awake, tomorrow."

«"Goodnight", murmured Rossini, before falling beatifically asleep. I paced my study for a long time, sipping excellent black coffee... Then, when God willed it, I was able to draft the sketch I had been asked for and send it to Rossini in the morning».

Gioachino was again composing and was surrounded by his noisy friends. A month later the opera was staged and on opening night it met with the same difficulties that had accompanied the appearance of the *Barbiere*. Then, just as promptly, the opera was resuscitated.

Cenerentola inspired in Rossini accents of sweetness not repeated in the operas that followed it. «Candor, mischievousness, and devilish rhythm», Riccardo Bacchelli wrote in more recent times, «in *Cenerentola* are the source of irresistible musical inventions. Swept out of the real world, we are carried away by a tornado in which fairy-tale and farce become sound and poetry».

In the 1960s, an American oboeist told Maestro Alberto Zedda that certain passages of *Barbiere* and *Cenerentola* were impossible to execute if one observed the tempos he requested. The Maestro discovered from the original manuscript in Bologna that the passages were written for the clarinet. This set off the critical revision of Rossini's works. Thus arose a new interpretative awareness.

La Gazza Ladra *(on right) and the "Mohammed's tent" (below) in the "Collection of Stage Sets" by Alessandro Sanquirico, 1830. Below: frontispiece of the libretto of* La Gazza Ladra, *produced at Lucca, 1818.*

LA
GAZZA LADRA
MELODRAMMA

DA RAPPRESENTARSI

IN LUCCA
·
NEL REGIO TEATRO PANTERA

L'autunno del 1818.

LUCCA

PRESSO BENEDINI E ROCCHI

Con Approvazione.

HOW TO COMPOSE
AN OVERTURE

In 1817, Rossini showed up again at La Scala with *La Gazza Ladra* (The Thieving Magpie). This was the real life story of a housemaid accused of having stolen a silver fork, which in fact had been snatched up by the bizarre bird. Only after the girl had fallen in front of the firing squad was the fork recovered from the bird's nest. But the libretto set to music by Gioachino had a happy ending.

La Gazza Ladra was one of the greatest successes of his career: There were endless ovations. Many years later, to a young man who had written him to ask what was the best way to compose an overture, the Maestro had replied: «Wait until the evening of the day before opening night. Nothing is a better goad to inspiration than necessity, than the presence of a copyist waiting for your work. I composed the overture to *La Gazza Ladra* on the day of the première, right under the roof of La Scala, where I was imprisoned by the manager, watched over by four stagehands who had orders to hand my manuscript pages, one by one, to the copyist waiting below to transcribe them. In case there were't any music sheets, they had orders to throw me out the window. For *Il Barbiere* I did even better: I did not compose an overture at all, and used one that was meant for another opera. The public was more than satisfied. I composed the overture for *Le Comte Ory* while fishing, with my feet in the water and in the company of the Spanish financier Aguado, who was telling me all about his country's financial affairs. The overture for *Guillaume Tell* was composed under more or less similar conditions. As for *Mosé*, I didn't do one».

Bombs, cannon, bells, trumpets, anvils hammered on and even a musical douche to celebrate humourously the overwhelming sonority of the Rossinian overture. This is the first page of the satiric magazine "Hanneton", published in Paris for the Maestro's seventy-fifth birthday. Alongside: frontispiece of the overture for Turco in Italia.

NEAPOLITAN LIGHTS AND SHADOWS

The very human and intimate dimension of *La Gazza Ladra* was followed by a huge, Bible-inspired fresco: *Mosè in Egitto* (Moses in Egypt). Its libretto was the work of the Neapolitan poet Leone Tottola, whose unkind description by a contemporary runs approximately as follows:

«Of Tottola librettist, we know that
He is certainly no eagle, but a bat».

which in Italian rhymes the name Tottola with *nottola*, the word for bat.

Praise of *Mosè in Egitto* at the Teatro San Carlo in Naples was unanimous. Even Wagner complimented Rossini on it. The last scene, however, did not seem to elicit the desired emotions, perhaps because the legs of the stagehands were visible beneath the waves of the Red Sea. Finally, Tottola rushed up to Gioachino crying: «I've saved the third act! It took me just an hour to

Above: a moment from La Donna del Lago, *staged at the Rossini Opera Festival at Pesaro in 1981. Left: the mezzo-soprano Maria Teresa Belloc-Giorgi in the same opera, 1820. The singer was also the first interpreter of* L'Inganno Felice *and* La Gazza Ladra. *Right and on the opposite page: some scenes from* Il Barbiere di Siviglia, *staged with marionettes from the Salzburger Marionettentheater.*

write a prayer for the crossing of the sea!». «If you wrote a prayer in an hour», the Maestro said, «I will compose the music in ten minutes». And that is how the invocation "Dal tuo stellato soglio" (From your star-studden throne), came to be created.

Rossini's other Neapolitan operas, *La Gazzetta* (The Gazette), *Armida, Zoraide, La Donna del Lago* (The Lady of the Lake), *Ermione, Maometto II,* and *Zelmira*, were not always equally successful now because he was exploring new paths and did not seem sufficiently "Rossinian" to the Neapolitans audience.

A young French composer, Desiré Alexandre Batton, suggested to the Maestro the subject for a new opera. He had read Sir Walter Scott's "The Lady of the Lake" and had thought of turning it into a libretto for himself. Rossini said to him: «Lend me that book, I want to see if I can use it myself». Two days later, Gioachino affectionately hugged his young friend, announcing that he liked the story very much and that he would ask Tottola to put it in verse. Like Byron, Scott now filled the air of half of Europe. On the opening nigth of *La Donna del Lago*, the audience applauded only Colbran's final rondo, which distressed Rossini. By the second night the opera recovered and the experts were proclaiming that «anyone who is not familiar with *La Donna del Lago* cannot say he knows Rossini». After hearing the opera in Rome, the poet Giacomo Lepoardi said: «I, too, might weep if the gift of tears were not denied me».

Massimo d'Azeglio painted his self-portrait against the background of the auditorium and stage of Milan's largest theater in a picture preserved in Rome's Gallery of Modern Art. Painter and literary man, the future son-in-law of Alessandro Manzoni, whose daughter Giulia he married and the future president of the Council of the King of Sardinia, when he was young d'Azeglio had an eventful and lively life. His relations with Rossini and a hoax he perpetrated together with Rossini are described in his Memoirs.

ROSSINI, PAGANINI AND MASSIMO D'AZEGLIO

The painter and future President of the Council of the King of Sardinia, Massimo d'Azeglio, said in 1821: «Paganini and Rossini were in Rome... and in the evening I would often get together with them and other crazy friends of our own age. Carnival was approaching and we decided to get dressed up like blind beggars and go about singing for alms. We threw together four bad lines that said:

Born into blindness
we live by your kindness
On this day of gaiety
Do not deny us charity.

«Rossini set them to music and made us rehearse them over and over until finally on *mardi gras* we were on. Rossini and Paganini formed the orchestra, picking away at two guitars, and they decided to disguise themselves as women. Rossini tastefully added to his already bulging figure. But Paganini, thin as the neck of a violin, looked twice as skinny and lank in a woman's dress.»

«I can assure you, we were a tremendous success, first in the two or three houses where we went to sing, then on the Corso, and finally, late at night, at the banquet».

After the memorable fiascos of *Il Barbiere* and *La Cenerentola*, this was the only time the Romans applauded a Rossini premiere. However, this did not prevent him from loving the solemn Rome of the Caesars and the splendidly sumptuous Rome of the Popes, with its churches, villas, fountains and passionate, unpredictable audiences.

Another painting by Massimo d'Azeglio depicting the Roman carnival (on the right). Above, on the left: the portrait of the thirty-year-old Gioachino Rossini, painted by Vincenzo Camuccini, in La Scala's Theatrical Museum. Above, on the right: Nicolò Paganini, the famous violinist and a friend of both Rossini and d'Azeglio in the hoax described by d'Azeglio (oil painting by Andrea Cefaly at the San Pietro a Maiella Conservatory of Music in Naples).

FROM NAPLES TO VIENNA

The Neapolitan years were coming to a close. Throughout his life, Rossini cherished the memory of that enchanting city, its people, its theaters, its cultivated, genteel society. His departure also signaled the end of the bond in which love and friendship, ideals and interests, were ambiguously intertwined. The time had come for him to make his appearance on the international scene. Barbaja was about to become impresario at Vienna's Kärtnertor Theater. This was not a definitive desertion, but meant a certain loss of interest in the past. At the same time, he granted Rossini complete freedom to accept other commitments without any prejudice to possible future collaborations. He also let Rossini take along Isabella Colbran, whose imminent decline he was perhaps more aware of than the Maestro.

With the greatest concentration and intensity, the Maestro set to work on what was to be his farewell to Naples and his passport to Vienna. The faithful Tottola based the new opera's libretto on a tragedy by Dormont de Belloy. Many years later, Radiciotti wrote: «A collection of false concepts, commonplaces, strained situations which definitely did not improve in the hands of the Neapolitan librettist...». «Rossini devoted himself to the opera so sedulously that his spontaneity and melodic fluency were compromised», the same scholar added.

Zelmira was nevertheless well received at the Teatro San Carlo on February 16, 1822, a few days before the Maestro's thirtieth birthday. On March 6th, King Ferdinand attended the opera's final repeat performance. The newspaper 'Il Giornale' wrote: «The author and singers were called back on stage many times and an enthusiastic audience gave them the kind of send-off

Views of Vienna and Naples in 19th century prints. Above: the Graben. At center: the famous An der Wien Theater. Below: the façade of the San Carlo Theater in Naples, in which Rossini staged about ten "Neapolitan" operas.

Vienna's magnificence. To the side: the Belvedere Palace, built by Eugenio of Savoy and (below) a salon. Rossini went to the Austrian capital in 1822, summoned by Barbaja who had become impresario of the Kärtnertortheater, to help in the staging of Zelmira. *Below, at left: Rossini's "signature" in a letter sent to a friend in Milan.*

which is the most yearned-for reward of generous spirits».

A few months before, on December 14, 1821, Rossini had written to his uncle Giuseppe Guidarini (the brother of the uncle who wanted to have him castrated) asking him for his confirmation certificate and a document stating that he was single, in order to marry Isabella Colbran. Perhaps he would have preferred to remain a bachelor, but his mother's desire to put an end to malicious gossip may have encouraged him to marry. The wedding took place in the intimacy of Castenaso near Bologna, where Isabella had a villa. In the marriage contract Gioachino was assigned all the income and half ownership of Isabella's properties near Bologna and also in Sicily, which amounted to forty thousand *scudi*. After a brief stay in Castenaso, the newlyweds continued on their way to Vienna where a Rossini festival was being prepared.

Vienna looked solemn and festive to Gioachino, and endowed with extraordinary warmth for a northern city. *Zelmira* opened on April 12th and the production was excellent, despite the fact that Colbran's voice left much to be desired.

ROSSINI, SALIERI AND BEETHOVEN

A view of Vienna in a painting by Bernardo Bellotto. Rossini arrived in that city, the unquestionable capital of music, in March 1822, immediately after his marriage to Isabella Colbran. He had an encounter with Beethoven and was deeply moved by the grim poverty in which that great man lived and worked.

The only man who inspired in him a profound sense of humility was Beethoven. Here is the description of his visit to the great man, as Rossini told it to Wagner.

«I had already heard Beethoven's quartets and sonatas in Milan, and you can imagine how impressed I was by them. In Vienna I heard the *Eroica* for the first time and after that I had only one thought: to meet that incomparable genius, to see him close-up, even only once. So I turned to Salieri, who had been one of his teachers. He told me that he saw Beethoven now and then but that because of his shy and gruff temperament it would not be easy to get him to agree.[1]

«'Perhaps it's because of his instinct for selfpreservation', I remarked with a smile, 'that Beethoven would rather not sit at table with you. Or else you might send him for a walk in the nether world, as you already did with Mozart.'

«'Do I really look like a poisoner?' Salieri asked.

«'No,' I retorted, 'you look more like a big p...,' which is exactly what he was. The poor devil was not in the least concerned about his reputation

of having murdered Mozart. What he really could not get over was the opinion of a Viennese journalist who accused him of having scraped the bottom of his inspiration with *Les Danaïdes*, though without great efforts since there never had been very much in that barrel anyway.

«Salieri spoke to Carpani, a poet Beethoven liked and after much insistence the latter got the invitation. As I climbed the stairs to his poor lodgings, I could scarcely control my emotions. When the door opened I found myself in a filthy and horrendously cluttered attic. The room, right below the roof, had wide cracks in its ceiling through which the rain must have poured in torrents.

«No portrait could ever reproduce the indefinable sadness that emanated from his features, while below his thick eyebrows, almost cavernous, glittered his small but piercing eyes. Beethoven complimented me for the *Barbiere* and advised me not to go against nature by writing other things, because Italians do not possess sufficient musical knowledge to write true dra-

Below: portraits of Beethoven and Salieri. Antonio Salieri was a composer at the Court in Vienna and a music teacher. He had among his students Beethoven himself, Schubert and Liszt. Rossini turned to him to get an introduction to the Maestro from Bonn.

Below: another view of Vienna with the Schwarzspanierhaus where Beethoven lived during his last days. Accustomed to changing his house frequently, Beethoven, at the time of his meeting with Rossini, lived at Phargasse, Faubourg Lehngrube.

ma. (I made sure to repeat this remark to Salieri. He bit his lips – but without much damage to himself, I suppose. He was so cowardly that the King of Hades, in the other world, in order to avoid the shameful job of roasting such a fool, must have sent him to be grilled elsewhere).

«Since in those days Beethoven was already completely deaf, Carpani scribbled it all down in German. He pointed out that besides my comic opera I had composed *Tancredi*, *Otello* and *Mosè*! 'I read those scores', Beethoven answered. 'But how could you acquire the musical knowledge needed for drama, in your country? In comic opera you are unequalled. You were destined to it by the vivacity of your temperament and by your very language. Take Cimarosa, take Pergolesi. In the latter's *Stabat Mater*, I grant you, there is much deep feeling. But the form lacks variety and the effect is monotonous. *La Serva Padrona*, on the other hand...'

«I told the Maestro of all my admiration and my gratitude for his giving me the opportunity to express it to him.

'*Un povero infelice!*' (A poor unhappy man) Beethoven replied in Italian.

«I wept as I descended the stairs of that poor house and that evening at a dinner given by Metternich, still deeply disturbed by my encounter and that lugubrious '*Un povero infelice*' which rang in my ears, I could not overcome a sense of confusion at seeing myself treated with such high regard by that brilliant gathering. I was unable to contain my emotions at the great man's wretchedness and my indignation at the indifference of the court and aristocracy to the sufferings of the epoch's greatest man. Their answer was the same as the one I had received from Carpani: he is the one who wants things this way. He is misanthropic and morose and would not know how to preserve a friendship.

«After dinner, there was a reception which brought to Metternich's salon the finest names in the Viennese aristocracy. A new Beethoven trio was played, listened to in religious silence and crowned by a splendid success. At that I made the proposal of a subscription to create an annuity for Beethoven, or to buy a house for him. 'You don't really know Beethoven', I was told. 'If he had a house today, he'd sell it tomorrow. He would never get used to living in one place, for he feels the need to change his lodgings every six months and his servant every six weeks'».

1) Rossini has given four contradictory versions of his visit to Beethoven, so much so as to give some people the idea that it never took place.

THE GOD OF HARMONY

Vienna conquered Rossini with the warmth of its hospitality but also with its delicious and varied cuisine. It was not in vain that the Austrian capital had been the meeting place of many different civilizations, which left their traces in all fields; from the German and Bohemian all the way to the Italian, which is sometimes echoed by the divine Mozart. According to refined gourmets, Austrian cooking even retains a memory of a remote Turkish presence. So it is no wonder that at the end of his stay Rossini's shapely protuberance, so well described by Massimo d'Azeglio, had become even more accentuated.

At the end of a gala dinner in his honor, Rossini was presented on a silver platter with a gift of three thousand five hundred ducats – 'with the entreaty not to be disdainful of this puny token of appreciation for the delightful evenings offered us by your music'. The Maestro said: «I returned the compliment with an "Adieu to the Viennese", a song with such limping verses that one might have thought that I wrote it myself...».

During a summer vacation at Castenaso, the Maestro was invited by Metternich to attend a congress of the Holy Alliance, which was to take place in Verona on October 12th. Metternich wrote: «Since you are the God of Harmony, we must have you at the congress, where the need for harmony is great».

Gioachino and Isabella arrived in Romeo and Juliet's native town about the middle of October and remained there for approximately two months. There should have been talk about love rather than harmony. Every balcony, every stone in Verona evoked the two young lovers' words. At a different moment and under different circumstances, Rossini would have found here the inspiration for a musical tragedy. Isabella, however, was scarcely suited to personify the young heroine and for some time now had become addicted to gambling.

A few days after his arrival, the Maestro received the visit of the Vicomte François-René de Chateaubriand, who headed the French delega-

tion. He also met and spent time with Emperor Francis I, Tsar Alexander I, the Duke of Wellington and other famous figures. For that solemn occasion the Maestro composed as many as five cantatas. The first of these he conducted at the Festa di Concordia. During the rehearsals he noticed that the word *alleanza* (alliance) coincided with a pitiful chromatic sigh. There was not enough time to change the music or the text. Metternich though was amused when Rossini told kim. A new version of this cantata named "La Santa Alleanza" (The Holy Alliance) was performed by the Maestro's before an immense crowd.

Surprisingly Rossini's greatest fault was a certain lack of courage and character. Yet with *L'Assedio di Corinto* (The Siege of Corinth) and *Guillaume Tell* (William Tell), both written in Paris at the height of the restoration, he was preparing to grapple with the problem of a romantic and popular theater responsive to the cultural needs of a Europe in ferment.

Opposite page, above: Maria Malibran, portrait in white wax by F. Tavaz, 1836. On right: Vicomte de Chateaubriand who in 1822 represented France at the Congress of Nations at Verona where he met Rossini, who was sent to the Veneto city by Metternich to compose four cantatas for the event. Below: two aspects of Residenztheater in Munich, Bavaria, the work of Cuvilliés, one of the distinguished examples of German theatrical architecture but realized in forms derived from Italy.

Rossini crowns with Semiramide *his brilliant "Italian" career. When he first started to write operas, Italy was still musically divided. As Massimo Mila remarks: «By bringing to Naples the innovations commonly in use in northern Italy, he carried out in music that process of national unification that had always existed in literature and was just then beginning to dawn in politics».*

SEMIRAMIDE

Rossini's last Italian opera, *Semiramide*, opened in Venice in the winter of 1823. He arrived there on a cold morning at the end of January. A fine mist softened the outlines of the unreal city. Then, slowly, the mist yelded to a pallid sun. The day was so pellucid and serene that it seemed arranged for the meetings of lovers. No longer the Most Serene Republic, but still glorious, Venice had built on own its ruins one of the most beatiful and prestigious theaters in the world.

The plot of *Semiramide* was taken from a tragedy by Voltaire. The librettist was the same Gaetano Rossi who twelve years before had written the verses for *La Cambiale di Matrimonio* (Marriage by Promissory Note). The reception was cordial and the opera ran for twenty-three performances. But Isabella continued to be a disappointment, both as a singer and a wife. It was only three years later in Paris that *Semiramide* found its ideal interpreter in Giuditta Pasta.

Many years later Eugène Delacroix, the great French painter, wrote: «What remains in my mind is the impression of the sublime which abounds in that work. Especially when I am away from the stage, memory blends the various effects into a single whole. A few divine passages transport me back to what I was in my youth. When Rossini first appeared, nobody noticed how romantic he was. He breaks with the old formulas illustrated by the classics in his time. Only in him does one find those introductions full of pathos and those swift passages which, outside of all convention, sum up a whole human situation. This is the only aspect of his talent that cannot be imitated».

Delacroix was exactly right. By taste and education Rossini would have liked to be the last classical composer, but his creative genius made him the first true romantic composer.

On the opposite page, scene for Semiramide *for the Paris Opéra, an etching from "L'Illustration Française", 1860.*

THE WHITE CLIFFS OF DOVER

In October 1823, Rossini and his wife Isabella left Bologna to go to London. On the way they stopped for a few days in Milan and for a month in Paris. Gioachino would have preferred never to have to leave that enchanted metropolis, where everything spoke to him of a fate which would bind him to it permanently. But the duties of a long cold winter summoned him to the British capital. He arrived in London on the 13th of December. His fear on the Channel was such that he swore never to set foot on a boat again, except for the one that would take him back to Calais. He stayed in bed for an entire week, recovering from exhaustion and nerves. The Maestro's name was just as famous in London as it was in Vienna and Paris. The entire city and the court itself were in the grips of musical frenzy. King George IV sang, the Duchess of Kent sang, Prince Leopold of Saxe-Coburg, the king's son-in-law and future King of the Belgians sang very nicely. During his convalescence, the King's Chamberlain called every day to learn how Rossini felt. On December 29th, the Maestro was presented to King George. The court band welcomed him with the overture to *La Gazza Ladra* and at the end of the evening bade him *Buonasera*! At the king's request, Gioachino accompanied himself at the piano while singing a comic aria followed by the aria of the willow tree from *Otello*, which he sang in falsetto, scandalizing the press because of the allusion to castrati.

After his presentation at court, almost every Thursday morning Rossini was invited to the palace by Prince Leopold, who liked to sing with the Duchess of Kent, his sister and mother of the future Queen Victoria. Sometimes the king, who had a mediocre basso voice, also joined these gatherings. Once during a duet he stopped singing and apologized for a mistake he made. The Maestro said: «Sire, you can do anything you want. So go ahead and do it, and I will follow you all the way to the grave».

Rossini conducted several of his operas publicly, and privately for members of the Royal Family, the aristocracy and financial world. He made a

considerable amount of money, which became
one of the bases for his substantial and well
administered wealth. On the other hand, busi-
ness in the theater was very bad. Plans to
produce a new Rossini opera, *Ugo Re d'Italia*
(Hugo, King of Italy) were abandoned and the
score vanished without a trace. A cantata was
performed in its place: "Il Pianto delle Muse in
Morte di Lord Byron" (Lament of the Muses on
the Death of Lord Byron), in which Gioachino
sang the role of Apollo. The cantata was warmly
received by the audience but the newspapers'
reviews were atrocious.

The Rossinis liked the subdued elegance of
London's palaces and the sense of insular assurance of its people. Then, on a clear summer
morning, on a calm Channel, Rossini bad fair-
well to the white cliffs of Dover.

After the triumphal sojourn in Vienna and the well-paid stay in London, Rossini, having concluded his Italian career and convinced of the necessity of a total renewal of his conception of opera, went to Paris where he remained for the rest of his life, rapidly assimilating the artistic *atmosphere of the French capital, so different from the one in which he had until then lived and functioned. Below: La Place de la Concorde in Paris; on opposite page, above, Parisian views from the first half of the 19th century.*

THE FIRST PARISIAN YEARS

Rossini and his wife arrived in Paris on August 1, 1824. The Maestro already moved under the sign of a destiny which would make France his second home. During the December of the previous year, before boarding ship at Calais, he had met a representative of the French Crown to discuss the possibility of composing a *grand opéra* for the Académie Royale de Musique (now the Paris Opéra) and a comic or semi-serious opera for the Théâtre des Italiens (the present Opéra Comique). His monetary demands, however, were so large that the French asked for time to think it over.

After less than two months, Prince de Polignac, the French Ambassador to London was instructed to resume negotiations. Rossini signed the agreement at the Embassy on February 24, 1824. On his arrival in Paris he obtained a further sign of the King's favor. After an audience with Louis XVIII, the Vicomte de la Roche-foucault, director of the Beaux-Arts, invited the Maestro to assume the management of the Théâtre des Italiens, even though this had not been included in the London agreement.

Few people at the time noticed that for almost two years now Gioachino's interest had been shifting from the stage to the bank vault. *Semiramide* was the last ray of sun in a day that had been even too resplendent. In the six years that preceded *Guillaume Tell*, Rossini wrote, while in Paris, two very successful adaptations of earlier Neapolitan operas: *Mosè in Egitto* and *Maometto II*, which became *Moïse et Pharaon* and *Le Siège de Corynthe*. A new work was *Il Viaggio a Reims* (The Trip to Reims), a *cantata scenica* composed for the coronation of Charles X in the historic French city. Also new, *Le Comte Ory*, a vaudeville based on an idea by Scribe and against the unusual background of the First Crusades, which to a great extent was composed of music from *Il Viaggio a Reims*, which its author had withdrawn after three performances.

Le Siège de Corynthe was applauded enthusiastically by a romantic Paris which had seen in the opera a clear homage to modern Greece's strug-

When in 1824 Rossini chose France as his second country, romanticism already pervaded the country's cultural life. The Maestro approached it cautiously». He wrote the cantata, Il Viaggio a Reims, *reworked some of his Neapolitan operas, produced his first French opera,* Le Comte Ory, *and finally arrived at* Guillaume Tell, *the very last stage of his adjustement to the new cultural climate (1829).*

gle for independence. The following year the happy expectations for *Moïse et Pharaon* ended in sorrow. He was told about his mother's death before its opening.

Rossini would not have withdrawn *Il Viaggio a Reims* if he had thought it deserved to be included in a regular repertory. This one act opera that runs for three hours tells the story of a journey, which never reached its destination, undertaken by aristocrats, dignitaries and gentlemen of various nationalities to attend the King's coronation in Reims. The *cantata scenica* closes with a huge party during which the national anthems of the principal European countries are amusingly paraphrased.

Professor Bruno Cagli, one of the most illustrious Rossini scholars, writes: «*Le Comte Ory* is the story of an erotic exploit, attempted but not carried to its end, despite the ruses of the protagonist who has recourse to a series of disguises, all in order to avoid being recognized as the terrible Comte Ory, who enjoyed the reputation of being irresistible to women. So, disguised as a hermit, a gallant lover, a pilgrim nun, he reaches at last the longed for goal, the threshold to the countess's room. But instead of ending up in her arms, he falls into those of his own page». «*Le Comte Ory*», Bruno Cagli continues, «is the opera in which everything is predestined to happen and nothing happens. On the threshold of a perfect conquest, the seducer is submerged in darkness, caught in a labyrinth without an exit. This is the work of a musician who has reached the peak of his ability as a composer but has lost faith in the possibilities of theater as a manifestation of reality, or a world capable of being represented in any fashion. The Count's impotence is perhaps that of the composer himself – he too is lost in the labyrinth».

«Having become a prophet, the composer chose silence and for only a brief moment did he allow his characters or, more precisely, the shadows of the comedy to speak on his behalf. And on the pentagram, these shadows suspended between reality and dream wrote the final key words: "La nuit et le silence"».

Some time before transferring the melodies of *Il Viaggio* to *Le Comte Ory*, Rossini had already chosen the subject for what was to be his next and last opera, *Guillaume Tell* (William Tell). This was and adaptation of Schiller's masterpiece written by the librettist Etienne de Jouy. And four months before the première of *Le Comte Ory*, Rossini announced that with *Guillaume Tell* he would quit writing for the theater. After the second performance of *Le Comte Ory*, the Maestro set to work on the new opera while staying at the Castle of Petit-Bourg on the road to Fontainebleau, a castle that belonged to his friend, the Marquis Alejandro Aguado, the Spanish banker.

Gioachino was now thirty-seven and no longer composed in the evening surrounded by his friends' merry chatter. He was worn out by fatigue and anxiety, the torments of a life that had every right to weariness. But before laying down his pen for good, he wanted to give a proud answer to those exponents of French and German romanticism who looked so condescendingly upon his past as a composer of comic operas.

The first performance of *Guillaume Tell* on August 3, 1829 was attended by a magnificent audience. The uninitiated remained perplexed by so much innovative audacity. But musicians comforted Rossini with their enthusiasm. Donizetti said that if the first and third acts were composed by a genius, the second was written by God Almighty. In the balmy forest of a legendary and idyllic Switzerland, Rossini sings not only of Helvetia but also and above all of his native Italy. Fifteen years after *Fidelio* and two years before *Norma*, he attains with *Tell* a musical peak and a national stature which during the second half of the century will be equalled only by Wagner and Verdi in their best moments.

A few days after *Tell*'s première, Rossini left Paris, looking forward to a long stay in Bologna and determined to leave music before it left him. Two months earlier the King's household had granted him a pension in view of his retirement from the stage.

Pictures and history of Guillaume Tell. Above, on left: a La Scala production with scenery by Salvatore Fiume and Sandro Bolchi's direction. In the other illustrations, some moments of the epic event in 19th century prints.

AFTER CROSSING THE ALPS

On August 28, 1829 Vincenzo Bellini wrote to an uncle of his in Sicily: «After the Parisian triumph of *Guillaume Tell*, the celebrated Rossini, while passing through Milan, called on the lady of the house I live in. Having learned that I was in the same house, he expressed a desire to see me. Nobody yet knew that he was in Milan and I was therefore greatly surprised when a servant opened my door to announce him. I was in my shirtsleeves and did not have the time to slip into a jacket. Trembling with joy, I ran to meet him full of apologies for my unseemly attire.

«'You begin where others end,' the Maestro told me. That same evening he went to hear *Il Pirata* at La Scala, and he returned the next day. But nobody saw him because he was hidden away in a box. He told all of Milan that in my opera he had found a structure and a completeness worthy of a mature composer. Yesterday, at lunch, I met him again, with his wife. He said: 'You must love, love very strongly, because I find great feeling in you.'

«Now, everybody in Milan talks about *Il Pirata* and Rossini and about Rossini and *Il Pirata*, because people say only what he wants to hear. I was very fortunate to have known such a great man».

Rossini had planned to stay at Castenaso for a long time. Old *Vivazza* did not feel up to joining him in Paris, and Gioachino would have found it hard to bear if, as had happened with his mother, his father should also die far from him. The "pensioner" was in good health and considered returning to the theater by composing an opera inspired by Goethe's "Faust".

A year later, however, Rossini was forced to rush back to Paris. Louis-Philippe's constitutional monarchy soon deprived him of all his privileges and for a time denied him his pension. Banished by the Opera, the Maestro resumed the management of the Théâtre des Italiens. His stay in Paris turned out to be much longer than he expected, and this was the beginning of his final separation from Isabella, who had remained in Italy.

Gaetano Donizetti (above) arrived and was successful in Paris in 1838, brought there by Rossini. The Maestro from Pesaro lived in Paris and was much loved, and also in a position of great prestige as director of the Théâtre Italien (below) and the Opéra (opposite page, the lobby of the theater).

SPANISH INTERMEZZO

In 1831 Gioachino was invited to Spain by his friend Aguado. A performance of *Il Barbiere* was produced in his honor and was attended by King Ferdinand VII and Queen Maria Cristina, whom he had already met in Naples.

The next day Rossini was presented at court. The King smoked uninterruptedly, even in the presence of the Queen. After the customary pleasantries, the king offered the Maestro his half-smoked cigar. Rossini bowed with thanks but declined the offer. «You were wrong not to accept», the Queen whispered in his ear in perfect Neapolitan dialect. «It's a favor he grants only to a few». Gioachino replied: «Your Majesty, first of all, I do not smoke and, secondly... I cannot guarantee the consequences».

Rossini was bestowed another favour by the King's brother, Don Francisco, who asked to be allowed to perform in a dramatic manner Assur's aria from *Semiramide* for the Maestro. Somewhat surprised, Rossini took his seat at the piano. The Prince walked to the far end of the salon, struck a theatrical pose and, to his wife's great delight, began to sing, accompanying himself with all manner of motions and gestures.

Rossini often left his home in Paris to travel to various parts of Europe. One of these journeys took him to Madrid, where he was a guest of the Court (below: one of the halls of the Royal Palace at Madrid where he had a meeting with King Ferdinand VII - on left - and his family). This was an experience whose memory amused and perplexed him. It was at Madrid that the Maestro was commissioned by an eminent prelate to compose the Stabat Mater, one of his last masterpieces.

Rossini mementoes: on this page, on right: a bracelet given by the Maestro to Barbara Marchisio. On opposite page: a key to tune his spinet (La Scala's Theatrical Museum).

Aguado introduced Gioachino to an eminent prelate, Manuel Fernandes Varela, who desired an autograph composition based on the text of the *Stabat Mater*, the medieval poem which had already been sublimely set to music by Pergolesi. Rossini hesitated for a long time, then allowed himself to be tempted by a fabulous financial offer. Despite bad health, he composed most of the work in six months. One here might blame the Maestro for not telling Varela that not all of the *Stabat Mater* was his work. He received from Varela the gift of a golden snuffbox set with eight large diamonds, and the promise that the *Stabat Mater* would never be published. Six years later Varela died and the executor of his estate sold the work to a Parisian publisher. A long litigation followed, ending with full recognition of Rossini's ownership of the right to the manuscript. In the meantime, the Maestro had been able to complete the score with music composed by himself. This allowed him in 1842 to break a silence that had lasted for thirteen long years.

OLYMPE PELISSIER

Gioachino had now been living in Paris for two years. By now his Aguado friends considered him a member of the family. In the summer of 1832, in order to shelter him from a cholera epidemic, they offered him the hospitality of a villa near Toulouse. To anyone who saw him in those days, Rossini seemed to be happy. He had found a loving companion to share his physically and spiritually tormented but nevertheless still relatively young years.

Olympe Pelissier was the illegitimate daughter of a woman who since adolescence had encouraged her to accept the favors of wealthy men. She was, however, able to rebel against this fate. She was loved by the famous painter Horace Vernet. Her beauty and intelligence earned her the admiration of Honoré de Balzac. Olympe's fate was not dissimilar from that of another celebrated woman, closer to our time, Alma Mahler, but she behaved with greater humility.

Antonio Zanolini wrote: «Rossini became ill in 1832 and Olympe insisted on nursing a health which was endangered by all the indulgences of an unattached man. Despite his gay and attractive appearance, he was often ailing. The slightest disappointment overwhelmed him. But he could just as easily be moved by joy, tenderness, and understanding. Not only did Olympe take diligent care of him during his illness, but she also knew how to induce him to avoid its causes».

In fact, the Maestro's depressive condition was aggravated by a serious, humiliating disease that we would rather not describe in detail. This, however, did not prevent him from experiencing with Olympe many relatively serene moments. He composed songs and duets for concerts, which became famous as his *Soirées Musicales*. But it was above all the Théâtre des Italiens, which the Maestro was still managing, that still led him to live his moments of glory and sudden tragedy.

At the Paris Opéra, drawings by E. Lami (on left) and anonymous author (below). At bottom: Rossini's letters to Giraldoni and to Giuseppe Pasta, Giuditta's husband, to recommend Mme Pelissier. Opposite page, above: society evening in Paris (E. Lami); below: "At La Scala" from "Strenna Italiana", 1844.

THE DEATH
OF VINCENZO BELLINI

On September 23, 1835, Vincenzo Bellini died in Paris at the age of thirty-three. So Rossini wrote to a friend in Palermo:
«I have the satisfaction of telling you that his burial took place amid general love and a pomp which would have been worthy of a king: two hundred voices sang the funeral Mass and the foremost artists in the capital vied with each other to sing in the choruses. After the Mass, we set off for the cemetery and a military band escorted the cortege. I can assure you that the crowd of people, the sadness depicted on every face, cannot be described. The weather was dismal because of the rain that never stopped all day long, but it discouraged no one, not even me, though I had been ill for several days. Everything was carried out perfectly and, still in tears, I had the joy of rendering to my poor friend the affection he had shown me».

TO MARIA MALIBRAN

A few years before Rossini had sent the following letter to a woman who was tied to Bellini in both life and art and who was also destined to end her glorious day on earth prematurely:

«To Maria Malibran

Celebrated composer, singer, player of instruments, painter, fencer, orator, etc. etc. etc.

«Dear Marietta, I called on you at home to seduce you and take you to lunch at Dubraque's, who improvised an excellent little meal, but oh God! the return of your servant (after I waited for a long time) spoiled everything since he told me that you were eating in the country.

Next topic: Baron Delmar would like to have you tomorrow evening at his Society to sing a couple of pieces; I warn you that this is not a concert, although it will become one for your piece; if you could make up your mind, you would be doing me a tremendous favor. There will only be Rubini, Lablache and you, who were born to be an ornament for every garden.

I embrace you with tears as always, your most affectionate friend,

G. Rossini

At your house, January 14, 1832»

Vincenzo Bellini (opposite page) and Maria Malibran (above), tied in life and art, were fated to have very short but intense lives: the composer died at thirty-three; the famous singer at twenty-eight, killed by a fall from a horse. The naive allegory (on right) associates their triumphs in an ideal Parnassus. Opposite page: picture of Bellini's two operas: on left, Sanquirico's sketch for Il Pirata; *on right, scene from* I Puritani, *staged at the Théâtre Italien.*

"THE POWER OF MUSIC LIES IN ITS RHYTHM"

Antonio Zanolini, lawyer and later a Senator in Italy, tells us: «On a lovely day in spring, Rossini and I went for a stroll on the Boulevard des Italiens. We wandered aimlessly from one word to the next until the conversation touched on music. I said to Rossini that I found in Mozart's operas and even to a greater extent in his a great imitative power.

Rossini: "This is a mistake that also professional musicians make very often. Painting and sculpture are imitative arts. On the contrary, music arouses man, makes him rejoice in the solitude of the fields, reawakens his deepest affections, cheers, saddens, and moves. But it cannot transmit to man an image of what he hears".

Zanolini: "And yet, when I hear Desdemona in the last act of *Otello*, my heart fills with tenderness because that melody imitates the moving

lament of an unhappy person in the act of praying".

Rossini: "Music can imitate only that which produces sound: rain, a storm, a festive din. Within certain limits, song can imitate declamation. But such a limited ability cannot be considered an essential attribute. Music is a sublime art precisely because, lacking the means to imitate, it soars above nature into an ideal world".

Zanolini: "And what about Haydn's *Seasons*, his *Creation*?"

Rossini: "If it were possible to imitate, nobody coulde be better at it".

Zanolini: "But then, what does the true expression of music consist in?"... (at this point a person of high rank, I don't know whether a prince or duke, approached Rossini to shake his hand and began to talk to him with great familiarity. I wanted to leave, but Rossini gestured for me to stay. People going by gaped at him and pointed him out to each other as if he were some amazing phenomenon. Others doffed their hats, bowing deeply, while he, absorbed in his conversation, paid no attention. I did not see a single person behave in the same way to that prince or duke. When the chat was over, Rossini came back to my side and we resumed our stroll).

Rossini: "What were we saying? Music's expression is not as direct as the images in a painting, but it is more appealing, more poetic than any poem. Speech would be empty sound without the meaning attributed to it by convention. In contrast the language of music is common to all peoples, because it is understood by the heart. Music produces marvelous effects when it is accompanied by dramatic art, when the ideal expression of sound is joined to the expression of poetry. Music is then the moral atmosphere that fills the space in which the drama's protagonists move. It expresses the fate which pursues them, the hope which animates them, the merriment which surrounds them, the abyss into which they are about to fall. And all this in a manner that is indefinable but so appealing and piercing that it cannot be expressed in words or gestures. This force of expression must be felt by the composer, there are no rules by which to teach it, and it consists entirely of rhythm. Musical expression is a matter of rhythm, all the power of music lies in rhythm"».

On these pages, some moments from Il Barbiere di Siviglia *in La Scala production of the 1981-83 season, conducted by Claudio Abbado and with scenery and direction by Jean-Pierre Ponnelle.*

MEETING MENDELSSOHN AND THE NEW ERA

In 1836 Rossini went to Frankfurt together with the financier Rothschild to attend a family wedding. The Maestro says: «We went through Brussels, Antwerp, Aix-la-Chapelle, Cologne, Coblenz, Mainz, and I think I never saw anything more beatiful than the banks of the Rhine. What an adundance of vegetation, what cathedrals, how many memories of ancient times!

«In Frankfurt I had the good fortune to meet Felix Mendelssohn, who was then a young man and who, to the talents of a great composer, adds the merit of having rescued Bach from the oblivion of over half a century by performing the *Matthäus-Passion* in Berlin. I met him through the composer Ferdinand Hille. I was enchanted to hear him play his delightful "Lieder ohne Worte" (Songs without words). Then he played an opera by Weber for me. After that, I asked him to let me hear Bach, plenty of Bach.

«Surprised, Mendelssohn said, 'But do you Italians really like German music that much?' 'I don't like anything but that, I replied. And as for Italian music, I don't give a damn for it!...'

«His growing amazement did not prevent Mendelssohn from playing admirably, and with rare pleasure, many fugues and other works by the great Bach».

In turn, the young composer wrote to his mother: «Yesterday I went to see Hiller, and do you know who I came face to face with? Rossini, huge and fat, in his gayest, friendliest mood. I have met few men who can be as witty and amusing as he can when he feels like it. And we did nothing but laugh. He is getting to be a Bach enthusiast. He admires Germany and says that the evening he spent on the Rhine he drank so much wine that the waiter had to take him to his room or he would never have been able to find it. He told us the most amusing stories, not only about the Parisian composers, but also about himself and his music. He showed an almost excessive respect for all those present, so that one might have been tempted to take him at his word if one did not have eyes to see the astute expression on his face. He exudes intelligence, vivacity and elegance with his every gesture and

On opposite page, above on left: a silhouette traced by Gioachino Rossini of the impresario Barbaja's profile. The drawing bears some words written by Maria Malibran, portrayed, below, in an oil painting by H. Decaisne, in the part of

Desdemona in Rossini's Otello. *Above, on right: Felix Mendelssohn-Bartoldy (water color by J. Warren Childe) at the time of his meeting with Rossini. Below: lithograph of Rossini and his musical creatures. Below: a train of the first half of*

the 19th century. Anecdotes about Rossini record amply and with a wealth of details the composer's reluctance to go on journeys by sea or in the uncomfortable carriages of the first railroad trains.

every word. Anyone who is not convinced that he is a genius should listen to him only once to change his mind».

Less pleasant than the encounter with Mendelssohn, and quite as disagreable as that with the English Channel, was Rossini's encounter with the railroads, along the brief stretch between Brussels and Antwerp. He recalled the trip with a piano piece called *A Small Pleasure Train* in which the first trains are fiercely described from the devilish whistle to the sweet melody of the brakes and the terrifying derailment of the convoy.

A POSTHUMOUS CHILD

In the autumn of 1836, Rossini left Paris for Bologna. His previous visit had been brusquely interrupted. His father, once cheerful and lively, was now almost eighty. But even more than his father, Olympe was in the Maestro's thoughts. His health was so bad that the rumors that claimed she was his mistress were scarcely credible. Furthermore, there was no divorce in Italy. A legal separtion from Colbran was the only, satisfaction he could offer Olympe.

During the winter of 1839, Rossini's state of depression, which ill health and his separation from Isabella helped to create, was aggravated by his father's death. The Aguado family offered him hospitality in Paris. He was just on the point of taking over the directorship of the Liceo Musicale in Bologna and had decided to devote to it all his remaining energy.

The favorable outcome of his litigation over the rights to the *Stabat Mater* gave Rossini the strength to finish the score. But his authentically creative activity had retired, together with the stagecoach. On one occasion he said: «I wrote operas when melodies came looking for me. But when I realized that I must go looking for them, the idler in me gave up the search».

The *Stabat Mater* had its first performance at the Théâtre des Italiens in January 1842, but Rossini's ill health prevented him from seeing it. Soon the work began its European tour. It was performed at Bologna that same year under Donizetti's inspired baton. On the evening of the dress rehearsal, the Maestro gathered enough strength to appear in front of two orchestras and say: «Gentlemen, I introduce to you a great composer and conductor. I have entrusted the *Stabat Mater* to him because he is the only person able to interpret it the way I wrote it». During the first performance and those that followed Rossini could not enter the theater which was made so overheated by the crowd. He followed the performance in a nearby, well ventilated room. Afterward, the Maestro appeared at the balcony to give a festive salute to the large crowd. The joy he felt was that of a man to whom a posthumous child is born.

Picture of the house situated in Bologna on Strada Maggiore, property of Gioachino Rossini (on left). Below, on right: sheet in honor of Isabella Colbran.

On the opposite page, above: portrait of Gioachino Rossini in the City Theater of Pesaro; below and on this page to left: page of program for the performance of the Stabat Mater at Pesaro on February 16 and 17, 1843.

PROGRAMMA

STABAT

DEL CAV. GIOACCHINO ROSSINI

DA ESEGUIRSI

IN PESARO.

Se le antiche città della Grecia poterono contrastarsi il vanto di aver dato agli uomini un Omerò, quelle della moderna Italia non ponno contradire a Pesaro la gloria di avere generato il grande maestro ehe dal vecchio e nuovo mondo salutasi coll'invidiato nome di ORFÈO PE-SARESE. Quindi la patria sua tripudiante oggi per lo appunto segna a caratteri indelebili quell'umile casa ove egli dava i primi vagiti, e dove inaspettate vennero a tentennargli la culla Erato, Melpomene e Calliope. Quindi alcuna volta lo festeggiavano qui transitante i cittadini; nel teatro nuovo direttore e moderatore lo acclamarono; a lui nell'Accademia le palme di Minerva concessero; di lui ne'pubblici luoghi la caratteristica effigie collòcarono. De'tanti suoi capo-lavori giustamente invanimmo; e non fu luogo al mondo ove la incantevole sua melode risuonava, che di un eco pronto e clamoroso qui

A. Conte dis.ed inc.

ISABELLA COLBRAN

Nacque in Ispagna Ricca di avvenenza e di grazia, raccolse plausi, ed allori teatrali qual egregia Cantante. Il nome della Colbrand fecondo di soavi remeniscenze è scritto nei fasti del teatro Musicale.

DARK YEARS

Opposite page: the "sortie de l'Opéra", a festive lithograph by Eugène Lami. Below: some singers who excelled in the Rossinian repertory: on left, the basso Luigi Lablache, the basso buffo Luigi Zamboni, the first Don Basilio in the Barbiere, *the soprano Carlotta Marchisio (La Scala's Theatrical Museum). Below: the outskirts of Bologna in a 19th century painting.*

In the summer of 1845 Isabella Colbran became very ill. Rossini went to visit her at Castenaso and came away in great distress. He instructed the servants to assist her and for over a month he received news about her every day, until he was told that she had breathed her last after repeatedly pronouncing his name.

The next year on August 16th, Gioachino led Olympe to the altar in the parish church of San Giovanni in Monte. He could find no words to devote to events which were neither sad nor happy but nevertheless decisive in a man's life. On April 27, 1848, a company of volunteers of the first Italian war of independence about to leave for the front gathered below Rossini's window to render homage to him. From the balcony, he was applauded but also booed at by those who criticised his commitment to the national cause. Terrorized, he moved to Florence.

Two days later, at sundown, Padre Ugo Bassi, an ardent patriot and a priest, gathered a large crowd in front of the Maestro's house and made a speech inviting him to return to Bologna. He said that whoever did not respect a man who more than any other had honored Italy throughout the world could not consider himself a good patriot. The Bolognese press joined with the good Father, who again invited Rossini writing to him in deferential, amicable terms. But Gioachino would have none of it and decided to remain in Florence for what would turn out to be the darkest years of his life. Whenever he was told he should go back to composing, he would burst into tears. He said: «I have worked my imagination too hard. Music wants fresh ideas. I am simply weary and hydrophobic».

It was Olympe who made the decision to return to Paris, trusting that a complete change of milieu would be salutary for Rossini. They left on April 26, 1855. They stopped for a few days in Nice, where every evening there was held a soirée in Rossini's honor in the garden of the Hôtel des Etrangers. Gioachino certainly was far from imagining that perhaps his serenest years lay ahead of him in his oldest age.

RESURRECTION

The journey took approximately a month—and did not improve the invalid's condition. In those days Rossini ate without pleasure, had difficulty digesting, even the slightest effort exhausted him. To Verdi who went to see him on the premiere of *I Vespri Siciliani*, he said: «You don't know in what kind of prison they've stuck me!»

But sooner than expected, Gioachino began to improve. To a German composer who called on him to show him a prolix melody for violin, he said, after leafing through the score: «Hell, eighteen pages! I never saw anything like it. Still, there is probably something worthwhile in it. Leave it here with me, and I'll tell you which are the sixteen pages that should be gotten rid of. If you must keep the lot, put in sixteen pages of *pizzicato...*».

Rossini visited several spas, with good results. The triumphal welcome in Paris and the splendors of Second Empire society cured him of all his anxieties.

In the spring of 1857, Rossini returned to composing. At the beginning of April, on Olympe's name day, he presented her with five songs, which were as many variations on Metastasio's verse: "Mi lagnerò tacendo della mia sorte amara" (In silence I shall mourn my bitter fate). But he was just as frightened by the theater as he was by the changing times. Comic opera was no longer in tune with the social reality of the era. A conservative in life and a revolutionary in art, he had indeed been the one who, with the musical and national language of Tell, had broken the pattern and meanings of a world in which he himself lived at great ease.

After 1830, Rossini's declining muse, overwhelmed by the eruption of the romantic wave, found refuge in churches and drawing rooms. And it was again the drawing room that listened to the feeble voice of his revived Parisian vein. Gioachino had a villa built at Passy on a plot of land that had the shape of a grand piano. His house was open to all the major exponents of French culture, finance and aristocracy but, first of all, to all European composers.

The villa that Rossini had built at Passy, near Paris. Below: costumes for Mosè and Eliseo for the Parisian production of Mosè (1852). Alongside: Laure Cinti-Demoreau, one of the most important Rossinian interpreters of his time for whom the Maestro wrote the part of Anaïs in Mosè. Opposite: Rossini's autograph beneath a lithograph by A. Lemoine from a photo by Erwin; below: the audience in the Paris Opéra applauds Rossini (French lithograph from the middle of the 19th century).

A CELEBRATED CONVERSATION WITH RICHARD WAGNER

In 1860 Wagner arrived in Paris to stage his *Tannhäuser*. A number of comments about the great German composer, which were as sarcastic as they were apocryphal, were attributed to Rossini. But a common friend, Edmond Michotte, the Belgian musician and patron of the arts, arranged a meeting between them, and this is the account he left us.

Rossini: «Like a new Orpheus, you did not hesitate to cross this threshold which was painted for you in such dark colors. Why would I denigrate you? I am neither Beethoven nor

Mozart, nor do I consider myself a sage. I do, however, think of myself as courteous and would under no circumstances offend someone who like yourself, tries to enlarge the boundaries of our art. As for despising your music, I would first have to know it, and to know it I would have to listen to it in a theater».

Wagner: «You are absolutely right. I must be heard in the theater to be judged. That is why I would like to stage *Tannhäuser*; but in Paris there is a real cabal against me».

Rossini: «What composer did not suffer from it? On the opening night of *Il Barbiere* I thought

they were going to lynch me. I was welcomed by Paris with the *sobriquet Monsieur Vacarmini* (Mr. Noisy). I didn't give a damn. I answered the nicknames with amusing limericks and grimaces, and I handed out *pizzicatos* and thunderous bangs on the big drum in my *crescendos* in return for mockery. And if you see me wearing a wig today, it is not because these bastards caused even a single hair to fall from my head. But that is not what I regret... Ah, if only I could have studied in your country! Perhaps I would have done something better. But let's talk about you. Why don't you compose something for a French libretto, like Gluck did and Meyerbeer, and as I did myself?»

Wagner: «I don't think that would be possible. After *Tannhäuser*, I wrote *Lohengrin* and *Tristan und Isolde*. For me each of these operas represents a step in the direction of the definitive form of drama. I cannot go backward. And if I were to go ahead, I am afraid that Paris would not follow me».

Rossini: «What was the point of departure for your reform?»

Wagner: «It was the poetic rather than the musical concept of the opera. But the moment I tried to enlarge the meaning of words by the penetrating addition of sound I found I had to struggle with the demands of the worst routine»

Rossini: «You're telling me? Grotesque librettos, the singers' dreadful feminine bent... But how can a rational development of the dramatic action be reconciled with the conventions of musical form? Nobody sings in that way, with the exception of lovers, perhaps».

Wagner: «Obviously, convention imposes itself to a great extent. But its excessess must be avoided. First of all, everything should be oriented exclusively to auditory pleasure. True musical drama cannot exist as long as there is no reciprocal penetration by music and poetry, that is, a double conception fused as if by magic into a single thought».

Rossini: «But in that case wouldn't composers have to write their own librettos?»

Wagner: «Exactly. Not to look too far afield in

the conspiracy scene of your *Tell*, I find declamatory effects which have a degree of spontaneity that could not have been achieved by another person».

Rossini: «That's true. That scene was done over and over again, in accordance with my instructions, until those conspirators became 'my' conspirators».

Wagner: «This confirms in part what I was telling you. Further extension of this principle will lead to a new and fruitful orientation of musical drama among composers, singers and audience».

Rossini: «But will this transformation which so radically breaks with the past be accepted by the singers when they are asked to substitute a sort of declamatory tragedy for their singing, and will it be accepted by the audience which is so accustomed to the same "old games"?»

Wagner: «It is not audiences who make Maestros, but Maestros who make audiences. As for the singers, they will understand that art demands that they transcend the limitations of their roles and devote themselves to a higher mission, that they add impeccable diction to the prestige of a masterful recitation, both noble and realistic».

Rossini: «This is a seductive prospect. But will it not also be melody's funeral oration?»

Wagner: «Nothing can exist without melody. But it must be melody free from symmetrical periods, obstinate rhythms, obligatory cadence. A melody capable of imparting its own precise outline to each character. A melody capable of bending to the poetic meaning, and at the same time expanding in keeping with the conditions necessary to obtain the musical effect, as the composer envisages it. You yourself have given us a sublime example of this in the "Resta Immobile" scene of *Guillaume Tell*, in which free singing, well accentuated in every word and

Some scenes from Moïse et Pharaon *presented at the Paris Opéra in 1892, etchings from the "Illustration Française".*

An important revival of the cantata Un Viaggio a Reims *was the production in 1984 at the Rossini Opera Festival at Pesaro. Conducted by Claudio Abbado and with the direction of Luca Ronconi, the spectacle, done again in Milan the following year, included a procession and a few stops outside the theater. Gae Aulenti did the scenery and costumes. We present some examples of these on this page and below on the opposite page.*

sustained by the breathing strokes of the violoncellos, reaches the highest peaks of lyrical expression».

Rossini: «One more question, Monsieur Wagner... Is the simultaneous use of two or three voices and chorus not incompatible with your reform?»

Wagner: «Nothing prevents two persons from experiencing the same emotions at the same time. As for the chorus, it is an incontestable truth that the masses can react more powerfully than an isolated individual to fear, pity and anger. One has only to think of that admirable fresco which is the scene of the Shadows in your *Mosè*».

Rossini: «Does this mean then that I, without knowing it, made the music of the future?»

Wagner: «The music of all times, and that is the best. Oh, why did you throw away your pen when you were only thirty-seven? It's a crime!»

Opposite page, above: scene from Un Viaggio a Reims *in the Milan production. To left: two of the singers, Katia Ricciarelli and Lucia Valentini Terrani.*

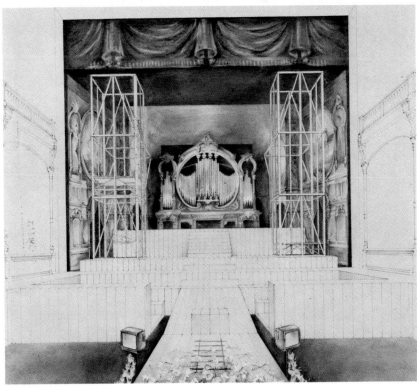

On right: Giacomo Meyerbeer, German composer living in Paris, is one of the major representatives of the type of melodrama called grand-opéra, characterized by historic subjects, sumptuous settings, ballets and rousing theatrical situations. He was deeply influenced by Rossini who became his friend. Below: the Rossini commemoration at La Scala, conducted by Giuseppe Verdi on April 8, 1892, drawing by L. Pogliaghi in the "Illustrazione Italiana" of the same year.

THE SINS OF OLD AGE

The pen he had picked up again after twenty years gave Gioachino the new joy of composing for his own pleasure and that of his friends. The minor works born between 1857 and 1868 add up to one hundred and eighty. Chamber music, mostly for the piano, which he described as *Péchés de Vieillesse* (The Sins of Old Age), often with semi-serious titles such as "Une caresse à ma femme" (A caress for my wife), "Quelques petits riens pour album" (Some trifles for an album) and the already mentioned "Petit train de plaisir" (Little pleasure train). Sometimes he followed amusing motifs with more important themes like "Dernier Souvenir" (Last remembrance) which was dedicate to Olympe as their final parting approached.

During those same years, Offenbach, whom Rossini called "the little Mozart of the Champs Elysées", included in his *La Belle Hélène* a parody of a famous passage from *Guillaume Tell*. Much amused, the Maestro reciprocated by imitating Offenbach's style at the piano. But since Offenbach had the reputation of not being exactly a bringer of good luck, Rossini composed his homage for four fingers, with the index and the little finger of both hands touching the keyboard in the typical gesture used to ward off the evil eye.

In 1864, Rossini published his *Petite Messe Solennelle*, which he called "the last sin of my old age". On that occasion, he wrote: «Is this blessed or blasted music? Good Lord, I was born for comic opera, as you well know. Very little knowledge and a little heart, that's all».

With its pared-down score, the unusual use of two pianos and one harmonium, the *Petite Messe Solennelle* is really a spiritual testament and perhaps even a suggestion for the composers of the future. Sensing that this was his last colloquy with music, Rossini softly muffled his voice which had been even too bold.

Rossini (above) in a photograph by Nadar in 1856. Alongside: the Maestro's autograph to the Marchisio sisters with the dedication "to the good God" of the Petite Messe Solennelle.

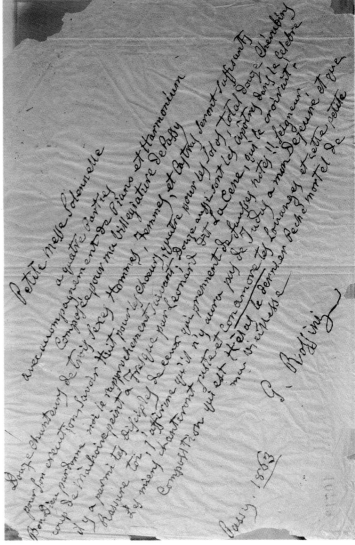

POPE PIUS IX AND MUSIC

The success obtained by the *Petite Messe* in a Parisian drawing room encouraged Rossini to compose an instrumentation that made it suitable for performance in a basilica. However, a pope had issued a bull prohibiting promiscuity of the sexes in the choir stalls. So who replaces the castrati and sopranos nowadays? Little fellows between nine and fourteen years of age with acid, mostly off-pitch voices.

After two years of hesitation, Rossini wrote to Luigi Grisostomo Ferrucci, a Latin scholar and librarian at the Biblioteca Laurenziana in Florence: «I would like to address to Pope Pius IV a respectful petition for him to issue a new bull that would permit women to sing in church together with men. I know that he loves music and I also know that he knows about me. A person who heard him sing a motif from *Il Turco in Italia* while he was strolling in the Vatican Gardens, approached him to compliment him on his beautiful voice. At that, His Holiness re-

Le Comte Ory was the first entirely new opera written by Rossini in France in 1828. (Here alongside: a Sanquirico drawing of 1830 with an outdoor scene). A recent staging was the one put on in Pesaro during the Rossini Opera Festival, of which we present on this page some photographs. Among the singers Cecilia Gasdia, Magali Damonte, Rockwell Blake, and Gregory Reinhart.

plied: 'Dear friend, when I was young, I always used to sing Gioachino's music'.

«If it is your opinion that I should turn to His Holiness, send me the draft of a letter – in Latin – of course. I shall be most obliged to you for it». Rossini received the letter he had requested from Ferrucci by return mail and he wrote back to his friend: «A masterpiece! You are my Virgil, let me embrace you… For fear of making too many howlers, I simply added the signature Joachim R at the bottom of the petition, which was all written in caps. Then I handed it to our Apostolic Nuncio, Prince Chigi, who promised to see to it that it is delivered into His Holiness's hands».

And again to Ferrucci, Rossini wrote: «Three months later, our Holy Father answered me offering blessings and tender thoughts, but the bull I am so anxious to see remained (I think) in his heart. Poor sacred music!».

DAYS OF EXTREME OLD AGE

In August 1868, the young composer Costantino Dall'Argine told Rossini that he had the "rash idea" of setting a new *Barbiere di Siviglia* to music and asked the Maestro "to afford my poor opera the protective shadow of his benevolence and allow me to courageously dedicate it to you, the author of quite a different *Barbiere*, in whose name I already felt universally condemned".

Rossini gladly accepted the dedication and replied to Dall'Argine the following words: «Your name is not unknown to me because the fame of your brilliant successes have reached me. I am very happy to see that a 'rash young man', as you call yourself, holds me in enough esteem to wish to dedicate to me the opera that you are just finishing. The only excess I can see in your letter is the word 'rashness'. I did not consider myself rash when I set to music Beaumarchais' delightful subject after Daddy Paisiello. Why should you be considered so for composing a new *Barbiere* half a century later?

«Paisiello's opera was recently performed at a Paris theater: a jewel of spontaneous melodies, of scenic wit, which was greatly and deservedly acclaimed. Plenty of polemics and quarrels arose between lovers of the old music and those of the new. You must go by the old proverb: 'While two rivals struggle, a third gets to enjoy the prize'; 'When two dogs pull at a bone a third dog snatches it', and I assure you that I would like you to be the one who gets to enjoy».

Sadly, for Dall'Argine the new *Barbiere* provoked a brawl in the same way as there had been fifty years before between Paisiello's supporters and Rossini's.

In 1887 the composer's remains were exhumed and transferred to the church of Santa Croce in Florence. On left: the "Illustrazione Popolare" thus depicted the event. Opposite page, above: the Maestro's spinet and Doré's drawing done on the Maestro's death bed; below: Rossini mementoes in the Olivieri Machirelli Palace in Pesaro.

NEXT TO MICHELANGELO, MACHIAVELLI, GALILEO AND OTHER GREAT MEN

Rossini continued to smile until the end. He closed his eyes in the house at Passy on November 13, 1868. Prominent people from all over the world and a huge crowd of people who loved his music and his personality attended the funeral. He was buried provisorily in the cementery of Père Lachaise, where Bellini and Chopin had been laid to rest. About twenty years later he was taken to the Basilica of Santa Croce in Florence, where he lies next to Michelangelo, Machiavelli, Galileo and other great men.

Verdi made a proposal that all contemporary composers write a *Requiem* in Rossini's honor. But the invitation was not accepted by anyone and the section written by Verdi, the *Libera me*, later became the ispired conclusion of the *Requiem* composed in memory of Alessandro Manzoni.

Today, more than ever, his music "soars above nature to fuse with the true expression of poetry", and it expresses "the fate that pursues men, the hope that animates them, the gaiety that surrounds them". Rossini will always bring the unmistakable message of Italian genius.

This picture, taken from an issue of "Illustration Française" of 1892, records the musical evening offered by the contralto Marietta Alboni, interpreter among the greatest of the Rossinian repertory, in her home at Cours-la-Reine, in honor of Gioachino Rossini on the hundredth anniversary of his birth. In France and Italy there were many celebrations with the participation of the leading artists of the period. Giuseppe Verdi, almost eighty, contributed to the celebration, conducting a concert at La Scala.

On the opposite page: the baritone Salvadori in the role of Figaro in the Barbiere di Siviglia, 1837.

ROSSINI'S WORKS

by
Marco Spada

Gioachino Rossini, etching by Filippo Pistrucci, London 1824.

CRITICAL ANALYSIS OF ROSSINI'S WORKS

VENETIAN DEBUT AND FIRST SUCCESSES (1810-1814)

A little less than three months separate the death of Wolfgang Amadeus Mozart (December 5, 1791) from the birth of Gioachino Rossini (February 29, 1792), a very small interval of time, an ideal passing on from one great genius to another of the task of guardianship of musical art. Very brief, but quite enough to regard the former as the very last example of 18th century civilization, aristocratic in the development and fruition of the musical product; and the latter as the initiator, despite himself, of the modern, bourgeois musical era, the era of salons and academies. Yet if it is true that all of Rossini's production is situated on this side of the nineteenth century, its roots still draw nourishment from the great musical tradition of Haydn, Mozart and Gluck, making the man from Pesaro the first Italian composer of truly European and supra-national stature.

In homage to a structural symmetry that can be considered the formal signature of his art, Rossini's career begins and ends in the name of instrumental and sacred music. First fruits of the lessons in figured bass and composition received at Lugo between 1802 and 1804, under the guidance of Giuseppe Malerbi, were the "Sei sonate a quattro" ("Six sonatas for four") which the twelve year old Gioachino wrote during a summer vacation at the villa, called "Al Conventello", which his friend and patron Agostino Triossi owned near Ravenna. The sonatas, composed for two violins, cello and contrabass, were performed by a group of amateurs who met in the Triossi home, and Rossini himself played the second violin. In the years to come he will humorously remember that he was "to tell the truth, the least bad". Despite the simplicity of their plan, the sonatas, all of them divided into three movements, show a surprising freshness of inspiration, together with a sure hand in the management of the instruments. In the allegro form it is still strong (reminiscent of Haydn), but the irrepressible yearning for the instruments' singing voice, which imitates the process of recitative in opera, is already clearly present, combined, of course, with all the rhythmic vigor of the mature Rossini. He will again use some of these thematic inventions (in keeping with a constant habit throughout his career) in subsequent works. For instance, the theme of the "Tempest" in sonata number six in D major, will be the point of departure for the "Storm" in the *Barbiere di Siviglia*. During the following years, which where spent studying counterpoint at the Musical Liceo in Bologna, on

vacation at Triossi's and on provincial tours where he performed as a singer at his mother's side, Gioachino composed many more occasional works. Among them are the two symphonies called *Al Conventello* and *Obligata a Contrabasso*, the three *Messe* of Bologna (1808), Ravenna (1808) and Rimini (1809), the Cantata *Il Pianto di Armonia sulla morte di Orfeo* (1808) and two symphonies, one in D major and the other in E major, which will end up in part or completely in *L'Inganno Felice* and *La Cambiale di Matrimonio*.

Yet around 1806 Rossini had his first opportunity to write an opera, thanks to singing-acting Mobelli family who, having heard about his talents, asked him for a work to include in their repertory. Thus was born *Demetrio e Polibio* (performed only in 1812) based on a makeshift libretto in the manner of Metastasio. The plot, hinged on an intricate dynastic problem, proves to be a repertory of commonplaces and stereotyped "effects", but all the same it allowed Rossini to move with dexterity. The shape of the work anticipates on a small scale that of his mature operas, and, if the overture is still tied to Hadyn's creative world, the vocal writing for the characters and the rhythm of the first clumsy crescendos are exquisitely Rossinian.

However, Gioachino's official career began in 1810, when his friends Giovanni and Rosa Morandi, respectively composer and soprano, obtained a commission for him for a farce to be performed at the Teatro San Moisè in Venice. The Giustiniani Theater in San Moisè was a small hall with not more than eight hundred seats, intended for the performance of short comic operas which did not require a large orchestra or the use of the chorus. Like all other theaters, it consisted of a staff of poets who supplied the librettos, chosen by the impresario, on any subject and for any composer. In this way a fledgling artist could test his talents. There, between 1810 and 1813, Rossini composed five farces: *La Cambiale di Matrimonio* (November 3, 1810), *L'Inganno Felice* (January 8, 1812), *La Scala di Seta* (May 9, 1812), *L'Occasione fa il Ladro* (November 24, 1812) and *Il Signor Bruschino* (January 27, 1813), stitched together on librettos by Gaetano Rossi, Giuseppe Foppa, and Luigi Prividali, taken for the most part from the contemporary French theater, which at that time was at home in the Veneto, or was inspired by it.

The farce in one act most often had a comic subject with elementary plots based on the eternal conflicts between guardians and wards and ending up in the obligatory marriage; but it could also be sentimental, like *L'Inganno Felice* in which are related the vicissitudes of a

young wife believed to be dead. Rossini had the opportunity to give rein to his creative talent and experiment with his personal concept of the internal architectural shape of such works. In fact in them is repeated almost unchanged a formal pattern that calls for the insertion of cavatinas (the characters' introductory arias) between the section of the introduction (composed of several numbers connected without *recitativo secco*) and an ensemble piece, trio or quartet, which acts as an ideal separation between the first and second part, a kind of small First Finale. The real small finale, in the form of a vaudeville, has the task of quickly stating the moral of the story. The comedy of these first works, tied to the realistic nature of the subjects, is fresh and spontaneous. The elements of Rossini's style are all there: vertiginous rhythm, variety of timbre, a light touch in the orchestration, and the characteristic deliberately scanned vocal line of the *buffo* characters used in moments of the greatest comic agitation. Rossini creates exhilarating effects of refined, never trivial comedy, allusive and never shouted, certainly an innovation when compared to the standards of his colleagues. Among the numerous jewels scattered in great profusion in these works, a place of honor is held by the overtures of *Signor Bruschino*, with the famous and characteristic tapping of the violin bows on the metal lamp covers and the overture for *L'Occasione fa il Ladro*, which is not a composition apart but merges with the following introduction. The five farces had their ups and downs: from the tepid success of *Cambiale* and *Scala di seta*, to the complete flop of *Bruschino*, and the triumph of *L'Inganno Felice*, which was the only one to remain part of the repertory throughout the century.

TRIUMPHS AND FAILURES AT LA SCALA

The first four years of his career saw Rossini immersed in frenetic activity. Alongside his contract with Venice, other theaters in the north began to engage him. On October 26, 1811, at Bologna's Teatro del Corso he presented a "gay comedy", *L'equivoco stravagante*, which was his first grappling with a comic opera of large dimensions (as many as eighteen numbers). The libretto's subject contains risqué situations, since the *equivoco* (the misunderstanding) is based on a switch of sexual identity between a young girl and a eunuch; the far from distinguished lyrics underline the situation with insistent and heavy-handed double meanings. And contemporary critics immediately pointed out its "indecorous idea", while praising Rossini's music which in truth includes some very delicate, subtle passages. It is interesting to note how in the figure of Gamberotto the "ennobled peasant" Rossini anticipates the more celebrated parvenu Don Magnifico of *Cenerentola*.

But *Ciro in Babilonia*, "a drama with choruses" performed in Ferrara during Lent of 1812, was almost a failure. And this time too it was principally due to the libretto, slow moving in structure and awkward in its verses. The music, however, has some very beautiful moments, which demonstrate Rossini's maturing talent and his attention to the expressive truth of feeling, though for the time being this is simply tied to each single page. Among them Ciro's prison scene in the second act, which opens with an instrumental prelude of great evocative power.

Thanks to the interest of La Marcolini, who had sung in *Ciro*, there were also opened the doors of La Scala, where Rossini had his first great success with *La Pietra di Paragone* on September 26, 1812. The two act pattern of *Equivoco* is used again and enlarged, but with a new and stimulating subject. *Pietra* is pervaded by a subtle irony that holds up to ridicule not only the traditional, aristocratic characters, the residue of Goldonian comedy, but also the new bourgeois in the "modern" professions, such as the journalist Macrobio. The elegant and civilized Milan of the epoch could not help but smile at seeing itself portrayed so mischievously. Here Rossini's music reaches its first peak of formal perfection and dramatic pertinence. Pieces such as Clarice's cavatina with the echo, "Quel dirmi, o dio, non t'amo", the song of Pacuvio, "Ombretta sdegnosa del Mississippi", or the first finale with the appearance of Count Asdrubale, in Turkish dress, who repeats like a man possessed the word "Sigillara" (with which the opera was identified *tout court*), must have had an enormous effect because of their musical originality and calculated theatrical effect. It is well known that the opera's success aroused the admiration of Stendhal, who declared that «*Sigillara, Tancredi*, and *L'Italiana* will ensure a posterity for Rossini».

Two years later the Milanese were not so farsighted when Rossini returned to La Scala with *Il Turco in Italia* on August 14, 1814. Its lack of success was added to that of *Aureliano in Palmira*, presented a few months earlier also at La Scala and representing the lowest ebb of Rossini's fortunes. The reasons for the two failures were undoubtedly different. In *Aureliano* the libretto again contributed; it was based by Felice Romani at the start of his career on an antiquated episode of Roman history; but there also contributed the uneasiness that Rossini by now felt about serious traditional opera, which was still focused on the conflicts of stereotyped emotions in Metastasio's manner. As a consequence, melodic invention did not succeed in giving sufficient life to colorless marionettes and remained caught in the coils of a somewhat rigid and repetitive formal structure. An exception, logically, is the independent, very famous and splendid overture which Rossini adapted later for *Il Barbiere di Siviglia*. Everything must

have been also burdened by the sluggishness of the performance and the crushing comparison with the already acclaimed *Tancredi*.

On the other hand, in *Turco*, aside from the initial resentment of the Milanese with Rossini, guilty according to them of having presented a simple reversal of the situation of the *Italiana*, the public and the critics did not grasp the subtle intellectual play that underlies it. In Romani's libretto (confronted here by an altogether different test), the character of the poet who, in search of a subject for a play he must write, tried to pull the strings of the characters (although in the end he does not manage to do so), in fact creates a meta-theatrical element that distances the audience from what is happening on the stage by filtering the events through a kind of lens. The apparent realism of the situation, with the bourgeois drawing room of Fiorilla who offers coffee to the Turk, is denied by the hyper-theatricality of the characters who indeed "play act" predetermined roles. Rossini's music, not inclined to sentimentalities, exalts in the rhythm's vortex the conventionality of words and actions by framing them in an alienated, exceptionally modern dimension, which certainly at that time could not expect to be understood. In *Turco* the structure of Rossinian comic opera is definitely established, with its internal relationships and thematic repetitions that tie all the scenes together in a coherent unity.

THE NEOCLASSICISM OF TANCREDI AND THE FOLLIES OF ITALIANA

But undoubtedly the summit of Rossini's juvenile production were the two operas written for Venice in 1813 at a distance of a few months – *Tancredi* (La Fenice, February 6th) and *L'Italiana in Algeri* (San Benedetto, May 22nd). With *Tancredi* Rossini created his first serious opera for a large theater. Gaetano Rossi adapted Voltaire's drama of the same name, producing a libretto well balanced in the succession of its passages, though it did not succeed in unravelling the tangled plot of the original, in which Tancredi's misunderstanding about the innocence of his betrothed Amenaide, unjustly accused of betrayal, is protracted through the two acts without her being able to explain the truth to her lover, despite her repeated meetings with him. Nevertheless the story's lack of verisimilitude does not prevent the action from developing with a certain clarity: the characters are very well delineated and the drama focuses effectively (very frequent in subsequent serious operas by Rossini) on the father daughter relationship between Argirio-Amenaide, caught in the conflict between support for the constituted order (country-duty) and a yearning for freedom (love). The character of Tancredi dominates everything. This adolescent hero possesses all the traits of magnanimity that makes him into a kind of Werther *ante litteram*. The delicate love story between Tancredi and Amaneide inspired Rossini to write the opera's loftiest pages; it is completely perva-

ded by a sweet melancholy and a serene formal composure which, wedded to the usual rhythmic vivacity, make it a masterpiece of youthful freshness. «In general the music of this opera offers a broken sing-song, but in each section is drenched in the most studied and suddenly brilliant motifs», the contemporary press cleverly pointed out. And the most famous sing-song was Tancredi's cavatina, "Tu che accendi", later known as the aria "dei palpiti" (of the heart throb). While at Venice, in deference to current taste, the opera had a happy ending with Amenaide's being forgiven and her subsequent wedding. At Ferrara, for a repeat performance during Lent of the same year, Rossini wrote a tragic finale that was faithful to Voltaire and concludes with Tancredi's death; but the very beautiful piece was not successful and only in recent years has it once again found its rightful place in the score.

Rossini's creative imagination proved to be inexhaustible when, in the space of about twenty days, having returned from Ferrara, he wrote and staged *L'Italiana in Algeri*. Haste favored the choice of a libretto written beforehand in 1808 by Angelo Anelli for Luigi Mosca, in which the composer made important changes, in particular eliminating the plot's more sentimental moment. Since the 18th century fables set in a Turkish environment were quite fashionable, thanks to the distance of these places and the mores of the people portrayed, they did in fact allow the author much greater license, which was accepted by European propriety precisely and only because of its exoticism. Thus subtly erotic is the story of the attractive Isabella who, having landed on the coast of Africa in search of her lover Lindoro, thanks to her cleverness escapes the bestial attempts at seduction of the Bey of Algiers and returns home with her fiancé. All the action is developed on the knife-edge of paradox with the comedy springing from the tricks that the "civilized" Italian lady plays at the expense of "barbarous" Mustapha, who in the end will be granted the honorific title of "Papataci", with the obligation to eat and not to talk. The culmination of the rapid succession of events is the first finale "Nella testa ho un campanello": in what is the most famous of Rossini's scenes of collective "bewilderment", all the main characters are carried away by a vertiginous succession of sound words (din-din, cra-cra, bom-bom) which in the wake of the weeping rhythm create what Stendhal defined as: "La folie organisée et complète". The opera immediately had a triumphant success thanks also to the excellence of the cast which once again included Marietta Marcolini as Isabella and Filippo Galli as Mustapha.

NAPLES AND SERIOUS OPERA (1815-1822)

The unsuccessful 1813-1814 season with *Aureliano* and *Il Turco* was followed by the fiasco of *Sigismondo* which was presented at La Fenice on December 26th of the same year. The Venetians, not incorrectly, considered the opera disjointed and weak, certainly old-fashioned when compared to the very new achievement of *Tancredi*. Discouraged, Rossini went to Bologna, where he spent a number of months occupied with occasional works. Here he received an invitation from Domenico Barbaja, the impresario of the Neapolitan theaters, to take over the musical direction of the San Carlo and the Teatro del Fondo and to write two operas a year for the next seven years. This was certainly a great opportunity for Rossini. He had at his disposal one of the most important and best equipped theaters in Italy, endowed with a great orchestra and an excellent company of singers. Furthermore, financial security would allow him better thought-out and conscious choices of the subjects to be put to music. But he had to defeat the distrust of the Neapolitans, to whom his music was completely unknown and who considered all "foreigners" interlopers. The opera with which he made his debut was *Elisabetta Regina d'Inghilterra* (October 4, 1815) – an "English" subject, which at that time was a great novelty.

Rossini again used a large part of the unlucky *Aureliano* and *Sigismondo*, subjecting each number however to a total revision both with regard to orchestration and vocal score. The first recitatives, as the Neapolitan custom required for the serious genre, were all accompanied. A transitional opera, *Elisabetta*, represents Rossini's successful attempt to free himself from the rigid approach of his previous serious operas in order to give life to an organic musical drama with a more coherent dramatic parabola. The bel canto finale has a new conception, with a marvelous number for the prima donna (proposed again also in *Armida, La Donna del Lago* and *Zelmira*), which will create a model for Bellini and Donizetti. The great Spanish singer Isabella Colbran, whom Rossini will marry in 1822, will be the interpreter of all his Neapolitan heroines, forming with the two tenors, Andrea Nozzari and Giovanni David, the formidable trio of voices around which the composer will mold his inspiration. *Elisabetta* met with the audience' favor and definitely established Rossini in the Neapolitan capital. Interested chiefly in the possibility for development of musical drama, during the seven years he spent in Naples he wrote only serious operas, save for *La Gazzetta* (September 26, 1816), a hodge-podge born purely because of contractual obligations.

In his choice of subjects Rossini aimed at novelty: from the rediscovery of Shakespeare with *Otello* and Walter Scott with *La Donna del Lago*, to the chivalrous world of *Armida* and *Ricciardo e Zoraide*, keeping an eye on the French classical theater of Racine for *Ermione* and on Italian contemporaries for *Maometto II*. Furthermore, he directly intervened in the writing of the texts, indicating with a sure hand his most personal and unalterable exigencies to the librettists Giovanni Schmidt, Andrea Leone Tottola, Francesco Berio di Salsa and Cesare Della Valle. That is to say the creation of scenes of ever larger scope, true moments of poetry that led to the invention of grand expanses of music; in particular, his favorite sections of the introduction, the first finale and a big concerted number in the middle of the second act. In *Otello* (December 4, 1816) he traced the delicate portrait of Desdemona in the melting "canzone del salice", (The willow song) a sort of ballad with tenuous vocal variations. What's more, he exploited the tragic conclusion to create one of the most dramatic duets in his entire production, "Non arrestare in colpo". In *Armida* (November 11, 1817), he musically juxtaposed the military world of the Crusaders and the softly sensual atmosphere of the "Isola Fortunata", where the sorceress captivates the knight Rinaldo. In the rondo "D'amore al dolce impero", in a profusion of coloratura she encourages the hero to let himself be seduced by the pleasures of Eros. But for the third finale in which abandoned Armida incites the Furies to avenge her, Rossini created a number of great expressive power with a completely anti-bel canto declamation, reminiscent of Mayr and Spontini's most "advanced" style. While in the first Neapolitan operas separate overtures are still being used, in the tragi-sacred action of *Mosè in Egitto* (March 5, 1818), Rossini deliberately renounces it in order to involve the audience immediately in the action. Here the opera's points of strength are the great choral scenes, with the seven plagues of Egypt, the death of Prince Osiris and the Jews' crossing of the Red Sea. This last scene, which at first aroused the audience's laughter because of accidents caused by the staging, in his revision for Lent 1819 Rossini interpolated Mosè's very beautiful prayer, "Dal tuo stellato soglio". The tendency to take importance away from the solo moments becomes increasingly evident by inserting them in a global dramatic context: no more static areas "of contemplation", but rather arias pertinent to the developing drama.

In *Ricciardo e Zoraide* (December 3, 1818), a tale of knightly passion set in Nubian Africa, Rossini wrote a "symphony and introduction" in which the two sections are, as it were, fused through the intervention of the chorus; and in it he introduced for the first time the very new effect of a "band on stage", that is, a group of wind instruments that plays in the wings. Also *Ermione* (May 27, 1819) begins with a "symphony with choruses", a lament for the fall of Troy which engulfs the listener in all of its tragic representational power. The declared Neapolitan experimentalism continues with *La Donna del Lago* (October 24, 1819), an opera with a delicate, pre-romantic color in which the misty Scottish landscape is a participating background for the amorous vicissitudes of Elena and her suitors. The choruses of hunters with the horns' fanfares and the protagonist's cavatina "O mattutini albori" with its cradling rhythm, reflect Rossini's intention of transfusing the music with nature's enchantment, anticipating the poetry of *Tell*. But *Maometto II* (December 3, 1820) is the opera that testifies most to the intense desire to augment the musical structure, which by now has become an enormous container of sections connected tonally and dramaturgically in an indivisible whole. Suffice it to say that the monumental first act contains only five numbers, among which is the famous "Terzettone" or big trio, a unique instance in Rossini's work. And also the second finale no longer has anything of the traditional Bel Canto conclusion, even sacrificing formal equilibrium to the urgency of the dramatic effect. The last Neapolitan opera was *Zelmira* (February 16, 1822), a darkling tragedy set on Lesbos, centered on the protagonist's filial love for her father Polidoro, who is dethroned by Antenore, lord of Mitilene. Here the structural experimentation of *Maometto II* is toned down; the classicist subject and the monolithic psychology of the characters again induced Rossini to shift his attention to the isolated piece, the richness of vocal ornamentation in the arias and cabalettas, and the richness of the orchestration. The Italian critics singled out precisely the "German" instrumentation, even though the opera had a fine success, which became a triumph when it was performed in Vienna in April of the same year during the San Carlo company's tour of the Hapsburg capital.

ROMAN AND MILANESE ENGAGEMENTS (1816-1821)

In the contract signed with Barbaja, Rossini had reserved the right to accept commitments in other theatrical "markets" so as not to lose his contact with the rest of Italy and also to have possible alternatives should any problems arise in Naples. Involved here in the area of serious opera, in difficult and risky experimental work, and at grips with the most demanding audience, during his various engagements in the north he composed mainly comic and semi-serious operas. After *Turco in Italia*, he felt he had mastered the structure of comic opera and was less hesitant about dealing with its content. During his first Neapolitan period, which had seen him prudently probe the taste of the audience with works "mounted" from previously written music, Rossini got into contact with Rome and Milan; here in splendid succession were born the masterpieces of *Il Barbiere di Siviglia* (February 20, 1816), *La Cenerentola* (January 25, 1817) and *La Gazza Ladra* (May 31, 1817). In Rome he had been engaged by impresario Cartoni at the Teatro Valle to present there *Torvaldo e Dorliska* (December 26, 1815), a delightful semi-serious opera centered, as usual for this genre, on the misadventures of a young girl pursued by a rich and powerful nobleman; all of this, obviously, with a happy ending.

For the following carnival season the impresario of the Teatro Argentina, Duke Sforza Cesarini asked Rossini to set to music a much more enticing text: *Le Barbier de Séville* (1775) by Beaumarchais. In other words, one of the most controversial and censored comedies of the last fifty years owing to its openly "revolutionary" content. The librettist appointed at the last moment to adapt the text to "theatrical use" was Cesare Sterbini, who had already worked with Rossini on *Torvaldo*. The composer insisted that he go directly to the French original, not only leaving aside the "purified" version that Giuseppe Petroselini had written for Paisiello in 1782; but also the ones that the poet in the "warning" on the libretto called the "many new placements of musical passages, which in any case were demanded by modern theatrical taste". On the plane of form this meant for Rossini writing the usual section for the introduction, first finale, etc.; but on the plane of content it meant accentuating the contrasts between Bartolo, Basilio and the Count, who at different levels represent the *ancien régime*, and Figaro, the concrete bourgeois parvenu, arrogant and self-assured, ready to intrigue in order to obtain the "portentous and omnipotent" metal. Rosina, the embodiment of the eternal feminine, mediates beteween these two universes with the strength of cunning. The paradoxical and grotesque humor of *Italiana* and the intellectual comedy of *Turco* here becomes the subtle play of the psychological ruses of many-faceted characters, who are reluctant to be enclosed in the frame of comic opera's traditional casuistry. Just as Rosina is anything but naive, so Bartolo is not at all a fool and will give Figaro a hard time before being toppled. Thus the barber's victory attests to the perhaps even brutal eruption of a new vital force in society which replaces the "conventions" of social relationships and the "conveniences" of economic relationships. The *Barber* was written and staged in less than twenty days, but the good will of composer, librettist and interpreters (among whom Gertrude Righetti-Giorgi, Rosina; Manoel Garcia Sr, Almaviva; Luigi Zamboni, Figaro) did not prevent the opera from failing miserably because of haste and incidents that took place on the first night. But not for long, since the success of the second night grew to the point of becoming an absolute triumph. Rossini's masterpiece sums up in itself and definitively crystallizes the genre of opera buffa, destined shortly thereafter to disappear forever and be replaced by the more evanescent heroes and heroines of romantic melodrama.

But Gioachino fixed the seal on comic production the following year with *Cenerentola*, also presented in Rome at the Teatro Valle. The libretto was entrusted to Jacopo Ferretti, and in this case too the opera was written and staged in great haste. Because of this Rossini entrusted several numbers and the secco recitatives to the pen of the Roman composer Luca Agolini. And this time too, in an evening in so many ways analogous to the first night of *Barbiere* (and again with La Righetti-Giorgio as Angelina), the opera "did not meet" with the taste of the audience, but it recovered immediately afterward. This is easily understandable: the Romans needed the time necessary to digest the shock of seeing Perrault's fairy tale, known to everyone, represented with features totally unlike the traditional ones. The story of the "brooder in the Cinder Ashes" had always offered other com-

posers the opportunity of turning the girl into a kind of "monster" of goodness. Rossini, on the contrary, depicted Angelina not only with modern traits but completely eliminated the fairy tale element by transforming the fairy into the pseudo-sage Alidoro, whose task it will be to accompany the girl to the ball. At the ball she will lose not the celebrated slipper but a more concrete golden bracelet. The "lachrymose" element is reduced to a very brief cavatina by Cenerentola, a litany immediately interrupted by the half sisters strident squawks. Rossini's abrasive humor does not dwell on sentimental effusions: all characters, good and bad, are leveled with equal sarcasm to the rank of marionettes who "play-act" a story. Because of this, in the finale the "triumph of goodness" is nothing but a pure vocal seal, Cenerentola's rondo "Nacqui all'affano e al pianto", which shows the audience that the happy ending by now is nothing more than a convention.

For his return to La Scala, where the failures of *Aureliana* and *Turco* were still vividly remembered, Rossini chose a semi-serious subject, *La Gazza Ladra*, taken from a recent French drama which was based on a real life incident. Expectations were great and Rossini devoted himself completely to producing a totally new work (without the usual textual borrowings) of great musical and dramatic complexity. The plot hinges on the unjust accusation levelled at Ninetta – the young maid of the "rich landowner" Fabrizio Vingradito – of having stolen some silver cutlery. Tried and locked up in jail, only at the end will it be discovered that the perpetrator of the theft has in reality been a spiteful bird. A story of so-called "half character" which would imply the adoption of musical mannerisms consonant with the "lachrymose" genre. Here not only did Rossini concentrate the comic element in the first act, but he reduced the pathetic to a few strokes. In fact the tones and style of serious opera prevail, especially in Ninetta's duet with the father, "Come frenar il pianto", in the first finale, with the girl's accusation and imprisonment, and in the true preliminary trial, "A pieni voti è condannata". The Milanese recognized the opera's importance and the press singled out «an indefinable chiaroscuro, which imparts greater interest to the passages». Among these are certainly included the overture or "sinfonia" which with its drum rolls masterfully establishes the drama's atmosphere.

After *Armida* in Naples, 1817 came to a close with a fiasco of *Adelaide di Borgogna*, presented in Rome on December 27 at the Argentina, written without interest by a Rossini already more deeply involved in the writing of *Mosè in Egitto*. During the following year he devoted less and less energy to the works commissioned outside Naples. In 1818 at Bologna he wrote several numbers of the farce *Adina*, which will be staged only in 1826 at Lisbon. On April 24, 1819 comes the turn of *Eduardo e Cristina* for Venice, a hodge-podge into which is siphoned music from *Adelaide*, *Ricciardo* and *Ermione*, but which has a great though ephemeral success. On the other

hand, the serious opera *Bianca e Falliero*, presented at La Scala on December 26, 1819, did not please the Milanese; essentially it went back to the pattern of the more important Neapolitan operas but with the reinstatement of the sinfonia and the recitativo secco. Yet Rossini's last semi-serious opera and the last written for Rome, *Matilde di Shabran* (February 24, 1821), was well received. The press highly praised the music but strongly advised the composer in the future to change his librettist, who was once again Jacopo Ferretti.

SEMIRAMIDE AND THE FAREWELL TO ITALY (1823)

Having fulfilled his Neapolitan commitments, Rossini accepted Fenice's request for a new opera. *Semiramide* (February 3, 1823) will be his last Italian opera before his definitive removal to France. The subject, which has a very ancient origin, has been adapted to the musical theater several times because of the great interest of its subject. The plot centers on the murder of Nino, King of Assyria, by the hand of his consort Semiramide, with the complicity of Prince Assur. By the will of the king's ghost, Semiramide will in turn be killed by her own son Arsace, who will ascend to the throne acclaimed by the populace. The tragedy presented burning themes such as incest (in fact Semiramide loves Arsace, unaware of the link between them) and matricide. These had already been endowed with classical composure by Voltaire, who had shown Arsace, in the dark of the underground passage, unaware of having given the death blow to his mother. Relying on this version, Gaetano Rossi wrote for the first time side by side with Rossini a libretto for the God-fearing 19th century audience. Conforming to the esthetics of classical theater, Rossini eliminated all offensive realism from the story, entrusting the most intensely tragic moments to a few exchanges among the characters, not commented on by music's "evocative" power. He put the Neapolitan experience to good use, trough he gave up the experimentalism of *Ermione* or *Maometto II*. *Semiramide* includes a regular "sinfonia" (whose theme anticipates several of the opera's scenes) and is divided into two acts of equal importance. The numbers are distributed with great balance and symmetry (especially in the duets), but they are dramaturgically aimed at pivotal moments in the action: the first finale, with the appearance of the ghost, and the "darkness" trio "L'usato ardir" in the second act. As he had already done in *Tancredi* and *La Donna del Lago*, Rossini here reinstates the contralto "trouser part" for the role of the male hero Arsace. In the fusion of the burnished timbre with that of Semiramide will be recreated those amorous "tender links" which only the music and not the words, subject to the official censorship, could supply. Thus it will be left to the vocal coloring to heighten to its peak the amorous sentiment between mother and son, but also to suggest the characters' majestic origin. In the opera bel canto is accompanied also by passages of great novelty, already projected into an imminent future, such as the "mad scene" of Assur, who, in the grip of remorse, believes he sees Nino's ghost, thus anticipating the vision of a ghost in Verdi's *Macbeth*; or the great scene of the oath in the first finale. With *Semiramide* Rossini ideally went back over the stages of an entire career devoted to the exaltation of the ideally beautiful, of sentiments both delicate and heroic, vestiges of a forever dead past recreated nostalgically for a present which was beginning to become ever more alien to him and will prematurely force him into silence.

THE PARISIAN COMPROMISE (1814-1818)

Considering the Italian experience concluded once and for all, desirous of new acquaintances and of ensuring for himself a financially secure future, Rossini decided to accept the offers that the Parisian Royal household had been making him for many years. After a brief sojourn in the capital in 1823, on his way to London (where with his wife Isabella Colbran he will stay until July 26, 1824), on November 26, 1824 he was appointed music and stage director at the Théâtre Royal Italien in Paris with a yearly stipend of 20,000 francs. The first work which – after much indecision – he presented in the Théâtre as a composer was *Il Viaggio a Reims* (June 19, 1825), a sort of scenic cantata in one act based on a libretto by Luigi Balocchi and written on the occasion of the Parisian celebrations for the coronation of Charles the Tenth, which in fact took place at Reims. It counted on the participation of the greatest singers of the time (Pasta, Cinti, Mombelli, Donzelli, Bordogni, Levasseur, etc.), who would impersonate the cosmopolitan guests of the Hotel of the Golden Lily at Plombières, gathered there while waiting to go to a sumptuous ceremony of the "sacred". But an unforeseen accident forces them to give this up and decide to go back to Paris in time for the king's return. Based on a simple incident, not a true opera nor really an occasional work, *Viaggio* offered Rossini the opportunity to write again, and for the last time, magnificent arias and duets in his typical Italian style; but absolutely new in his catalogue are the "Great concerted pieces for fourteen voices", which act as an ideal first finale and then the true finale, a very long number composed of dances, folk songs and hymns, an apotheosis of the monarchy culminating in Corinna's "improvisation", "All'ombra amena del Giglio d'Or", an evident reference to the symbol of France. The "royal" occasion certainly sacrificed a score composed of so much extremely beautiful music and Rossini withdrew it after only three performances. Later on he was to use no less than six numbers from it in his very French *Comte Ory*.

By now his attention was directed to the creation of a French opera; but rather than make his debut on the stage of the Académie Royale de Musique with an entirely new work, Rossini believed it more opportune, as

he had already done in Naples, to face critics and audience, who were anything but easygoing, with already written works which were refurbished.

The choice fell on *Maometto II* and *Mosè in Egitto*, which became respectively *Le Siège de Corynthe* (October 9, 1826) and *Moïse et Pharaon* (March 26, 1827). The composer decided that these two complex and sumptuous Italian operas were better suited than others to adaptation to the French stage. In effect, this meant: amplification of the number of acts, reinforced sonoral texture, obligatory insertion of dances, and revision of the vocal parts for the new company of singers (in *Siège* the transformation of Calbo-contralto into Néoclès-tenor), keeping in mind the declamatory requirements of the French language. In the case of both *Siège* and *Moïse* one can speak of a true and proper rethinking of operatic dramaturgy, executed with a view to the spectacular requirements dear to French taste. The two revisions shift the center of gravity from the plane of interpersonal relationships to that of collective relationships, relegating to the background the amorous entanglements of Pamyra-Mahomet and Anaïs-Aménophis in order to exalt the choral tragedy of the Greek and Jewish peoples struggling for freedom from tyranny. While, compared to the Italian model, that acquired greater dramatic emphasis and monumental embellishment, they lose some of the clarity and structural solidity of the original. Nevertheless, in changed times, the greater accent on patriotic themes, though it caused Rossini problems with the censorship, guaranteed his success with the public and critics. To this certainly contributed also the real beauty of the added, unmistakably Rossinian pages, which inspired the critic of "Gazette de France" to write the morning after *Moïse*: «This is no less than a lyrical revolution accomplished in four hours by Signor Rossini. From now on the French howl is forever banished: one goes to sing at the Opera as one sings at the Teatro Italiano».

Ready at this point to test his strength with a new opera, in the spring of 1828 Rossini had already chosen its subject: *Guillaume Tell*; but during the protracted elaboration of the text, anxious to revive part of the music of *Viaggio*, he wrote *Le Comte Ory* (August 20, 1828), for a libretto that Eugène Scribe had derived from an 1816 vaudeville of his own. The subject, enlarged from one to two acts, described the erotic adventures, attempted and never brought to completion, of the Comte Ory, a new reckless Don Giovanni, at the expense of the Countess of Formoutiers. The medieval atmosphere with its Boccaccioesque tone and the innuendos of the text result in a delightful comedy of errors, saturated with elegant humor, very far at this point from the more robust and simple-minded humor of Italian comic opera. It is exactly in Ory's languid and theatrical yearning that we recognize the hues of a crepuscular melancholy which beneath the brilliant surface is the opera's true signature key. The insertion of already written passages, wisely weighed by

the author, occurs without noticeable fractures. Superb among the new numbers in the introduction to the second act, "Dans ce sejour", with the chatelaines barricaded in the castle to protect themselves from the assault of the Count and his men; and the final trio, "A la faveur de cette nuit obscure", the acme of the action in which Ory in the dark of the Countess' bedroom, believing he embraces her in reality grasps the hand of his own page Isolier. Whereas in France the opera immediately won the admiration of the public and critics, even that of Hector Berlioz, traditionally averse to Rossini, in Italy it suffered constant incomprehension due precisely to that particular "esprit de finesse" of evanescent, allusive humor.

GUILLAUME TELL (1829)

Meanwhile the gestation of *Tell* proceeded amid many difficulties. The libretto, taken from Schiller's play, was entrusted to Etienne di Jouy, who had already collaborated with Balocchi on the *Moïse*, but the seven hundred line poem that he drew from it did not satisfy Rossini, who had it revised by Hippolite Bis. Subsequently, in the summer of 1828, he also had some scenes modified (after having already composed the music) by Armand Marrast and Adolphe Crémieux. Having gone through so many hands, the libretto revealed its lack of organic coherence, which was aggravated by the limitation imposed by the censorship (as regards references to the Hapsburg Empire and such words as "liberty"), and Rossini at any rate was still displeased with it. When compared to Schiller, the motivations of the text seem more blurred, especially in the figure of the protagonist who remains at the margins of the story and does not undergo a true psychological evolution. It is Arnold, the Swiss adolescent, who represents the true Schillerian hero, undecided between the attraction of his love for the woman descendant of the enemy lineage and his yearning for insurgence against the tyrant Gessler. Matilde is the most "positive" figure in the opera; in her can be found the most noble sentiments (for love of Arnold she will support the insurgents) and she also mirrors that Pan-like feeling for nature which pervades the opera as the metaphor of a loftier liberation. But here too the love story remains in the background, since the true protagonist is the Swiss people, a metaphor for all peoples. Here dances and songs act as essential connective tissue, dynamic and no longer decorative elements in which the few solo numbers are set like precious gems. A good example is the powerful scene of the oath of the conspirators of the three cantons in act two, formed out of the fusion of as many as three male choruses. The opera, divided into four acts, is preceded by a grand overture, also divided into four parts, in which the dichotomy between the scenes of nature and of insurgency is musically announced up to the very famous Allegro vivace which erupts with penetrating trumpet peals. In order to give cohesion to this gigantic creation, Rossini relied on various factors: the "pastoral" rhythm (three/eight, six/eight) of the choruses and the waltz rhythm of the dances; the orchestration entrusted to the timbres of the woodwinds, horns, harps, etc., and the use of the so-called "ranz des vaches", Swiss folk themes (from which he took only the beginnings) differentiated in their use so as to recall different characters or situations. Particularly important are the "ranz" of Gessler and those of the three cantons, Unterwald, Schwitz and Uri. But in *Tell* they do not create the "picturesque" ambience as much as they create what Verdi called the opera's color, certainly unique in all of Rossini's productions. The theme of nature emerges with all its forcefulness in the finale when after the storm – during which William in the lake shoots the fatal arrow at Gessler – there lifts up the grandiose hymn "Tout change et grandit en ces lieux". Here the Rossinian melody of an extreme purity, passing from tonality to tonality and from instrument to instrument, over the accompaniment of the harp, points to the reconciliation of the now free man with the primeval forces of being. *Guillaume Tell* was presented on August 3, 1829 at the Académie Royale de Musique after a period of wildly excited expectation which had driven the price of tickets sky-high. But the opera obtained only a "succès d'éstime" from the audience, while it was highly praised by critics and composers (Bellini considered it his "musical bible"). The cast included Adolphe Nourrit, Arnold; Bernard Dabadie, Guillaume; Nicholas-Prosper Levasseur, Walter; Laure Cinti-Damoreau, Mathilde; and Luise-Zulme Dabadie, Jenny; besides the great ballerina Maria Taglione who danced in the Tyroleans' *pas de trois*. The scenes, reproduced for the occasion from nature, were by Pierre Cicéri. The opera with which Rossini pointed out to posterity the path to follow, which with *Le Siège* and *Moïse* open the path to Halévy and Meyerbeer's grand opera, had cost its author an immense effort. In the attempt at adapting the well-spring of the Italian melodic line to the exigencies of French drama, Rossini had gone against his natural inclinations, creating a masterpiece in which, all things considered, he did not recognize himself. The impossibility of going further with this compromise, the idea of what the theatrical world would become a few years hence, and the many external requirements of an "industry" of melodrama such as the Parisian, gradually forced him into a retirement as premature as it was sad.

THE YEARS OF "SILENCE" (1829-1868)

Yet Rossini's silence in the thirty-nine years he still had left to live was accompanied by a great deal of music, by that daily exercise of the art which had been his "cross and delight" during the years of his juvenile craftsmanship. For a man who had conceived of life in terms of a theatrical event, the refuge in chamber or sacred music certainly could not have been gratifying. All the same his "private" activity has bequeathed us a large harvest of small masterpieces, such as the vocal collection of the *Soirées Musicales* (1830-35) and the thirteen volumes of the *Péchés de vieillesse* (Sins of Old Age), which included Italian and French vocal melodies, numerous piano pieces (among which the series *Quelques Rien pour Album*, Trifles for an album), and various choruses. A place apart is naturally due to the two materpieces of sacred music *Stabat Mater* and *Petite Messe Solennelle*. In them Rossini, unconcerned with any requirements beside those of the expressive meaning of the sacred texts, approached again the cultivated style of the past, the contrapuntal artifices learned from the beloved pages of Bach and Mozart, and the spiritual rigor of "a cappella" (for voices only) passages in the style of Palestrina. Though still – and for the last time – without renouncing the prerogative of song, the lyrical effusion of sentiments which through it can be transfigured into an act of religious contemplation. And why not? – also without renouncing that certain dose of theatricality which his nature either demanded or did not allow him to do without. The *Stabat Mater* was composed in 1832, commissioned by the Arch-Deacon of Madrid Don Francisco Fernandez Varela. But Rossini composed only six of the score's ten numbers, entrusted the remainder to Giuseppe Tadolini and only in 1841, during a peaceful sojourn at Bologna, decided to finish the work. In its final form the *Stabat* was performed at the Théâtre des Italiens in Paris on January 7, 1842 and was a great success. Instead the *Petite Messe Solennelle*, written twenty years later, was the spiritual bequest of the seventy-one year old composer, sick and close to his end. It mirrored the deepening of a profound religious sentiment in a colloquy with God that had by now become personal. The body of the mass comprises a chorus with eight elements and four soloists and an instrument group of absolute novelty, two pianos and a harmonium. It was performed for the first time in Paris on March 14, 1864 in the house of Countess Pillett-Will and counting among its performers Barbara and Carlotta Marchisio, the "dear little girls", as the composer himself called them, who had "given him new life", giving him the chance to hear in 1860, one last time before dying, the adored and by now distant *Semiramide*.

Taking his leave forever from music and shortly after from life, Rossini chose to end his "small" mass with a dedication to God. With self-irony and minimizing with apparent good humor his genius, («J'etais né pour l'Opera Buffa, tu le sais bien!») the God of harmony, the Napoleon of music, the Sun of Italy, rendered an affectionate but final homage to the good old times.

Marco Spada

The soprano Montserrat Caballé, the tenor Luciano Pavarotti, the soprano June Anderson. (Photographs: Mondadori-Lotti, Publifoto, Liza Kohler)

Gioachino Rossini (1792-1868) was one of the greatest opera composers of all time. The opera of his that enjoyed the greatest success, *Il Barbiere di Siviglia*, which he composed at twenty-four, represented a definitive turn, combining as it did the farce derived from the old Commedia dell'Arte, with a comedy based on character more in keeping with the new epoch.

Not more than thirteen years separate the birth of the *Barbiere* from that of *Guillaume Tell*, the forerunner of Italian national melodrama, composed in Paris in 1829. This admirable opera embodied the proud reply of the thirty-seven-year-old Rossini to all those who considere him incapable of dealing with the great themes of the new romantic era. It was also the beginning of a spiritual crisis, aggravated by a painful infirmity, which condemned Rossini to a long silence, interrupted only by the appearance in 1842 of his *Stabat Mater*. Yet, during the years of his regained Parisian serenity, he returned to music with *Péchés de Viellesse* and the *Petite messe solennelle*, a touching farewell to art and life.

1792 - Gioachino Rossini is born in Pesaro on February 29th from Giuseppe, "public trumpet player" (town crier), and Anna Guidarini, a singer playing supporting roles in the provincial opera theaters.
1806 - Gioachino is admitted to the famous school run by Father Mattei. He writes some symphonies, six sonatas for four instruments and some masses.
1808 - In Bologna his cantata *Il pianto di Armonia sulla morte di Orfeo*, chosen from among the works of the students at the local Musical Liceo, is performed.
1811 - *L'equivoco stravagante* staged at the Teatro del Corso in Bologna (October 26).
1812 - *L'inganno felice* at the S. Moisè in Venice (January 8), *Ciro in Babilonia* (Ferrara), *La Scala di Seta* at S. Moisè (May 9). *La Pietra del Paragone* at La Scala in Milan (September 26).
1813 - In Venice *Il Signor Bruschino* (January), *Tancredi* (February 6), *L'Italiana in Algeri* (May 22) are staged. And in Milan, *Aureliano in Palmira* (December 26).
1814 - *Il Turco in Italia* at La Scala (August 14); *Sigismondo* at La Fenice (December 26).
1815 - Rossini signs contract with the impresario Domenico Barbaja for some operas to be presented in Naples.
1816 - *Almaviva ossia l'inutile precauzione* (later, *Il Barbiere di Siviglia* at the Argentina in Rome (February). *La Gazzetta* at the Teatro dei Fiorentini in Naples (September 26), *Otello* at the Teatro del Fondo in Naples (December 4).
1817 - *La Cenerentola* at Teatro Valle in Rome (January 25); *La Gazza Ladra* at La Scala (May 31), *Armida* at the San Carlo in Naples (November 11); *Adelaide di Borgogna* at the Argentina in Rome (December 27).
1818 - *Mosè in Egitto* in Naples

(March 5); *Ricciardo e Zoraide* at the San Carlo (December 3).
1819 - *Ermione*, San Carlo, (March 27); *Eduardo e Cristina* in Venice (April 24); *La Donna del Lago* at the San Carlo (autumn); *Bianca e Faliero* at La Scala (December 26).
1820 - Composes the *Messa di Gloria* and *Maometto II* at San Carlo (December 3).
1821 - *Matilde di Shabran* at Rome, Teatro Apollo (February 24).
1822 - *Zelmira* at the San Carlo (February 16). Rossini marries Isabella Colbran. He goes to Venice and then to Vienna. On his return to Italy he composes at Metternich's request some cantatas for the Congress of the Holy Alliance.
1823 - *Semiramide* at Venice (February 3).
1824 - Sojourn in London. In Paris he becomes director of the Royal Italian Theater.
1825 - At the Théâtre Italien the scenic cantata *Il Viaggio a Reims* (June 19) is presented.
1828 - At the Opera *Le Comte Ory* (August 20) is staged.
1829 - On August 3 *Guillame Tell*, his last opera, is presented at the Paris, Opéra. He returns to Bologna.
1831 - In Spain he agrees to compose a *Stabat Mater*.
1832 - At Paris he forms a relationship with Olympe Pélissier.
1835 - His *Les Soirées musicales* are published.
1837 - He separates legally from Isabella Colbran.
1842 - He completes the *Stabat Mater*, which is performed in Paris conducted by Donizetti.
1846 - He marries Olympe Pélissier.
1857 - Writes piano and chamber music pieces which will be collected later under the name *Péchés de viellesse*.
1868 - Dies on November 13 in his villa at Passy.

Basic Bibliography

Bacchelli Riccardo, *Rossini*, Torino, 1941.

Cagli Bruno, *Le Comte Ory*, Rossini Festival Opera, Pesaro, 1984.

Radiciotti Giuseppe, *Gioachino Rossini*, Tivoli, 1928-35.

Rognoni Luigi, *Gioachino Rossini*, Einaudi, Torino, 1977.

Rossini Gioachino, *Lettere*, foreword by Massimo Mila, Passigli Ed., Firenze.

Stendhal, *Rossini*, Italian edition by Bruno Revel, Genio, Milano, 1949.

Weinstock Herbert, *Rossini*, published in U.S.A. by Alfred A. Knopf, Inc., and in the United Kingdom by the Oxford University Press. Copyright 1968 Herbert Weinstock.

The Publisher is grateful to Alfred A. Knopf Inc. and Oxford University Press, publishers of *Rossini* by Herbert Weinstock.

Illustration credits: Agenzia Ricciarini, Milano: 26a, 29a, 30b, 31b (Simion), 34, 35ad, 41ad, 42a, 60b, 63bd. Alverà, Roma: 8, 9, 11b, 34b, 37a, 37bd, 37bs, 40b, 41b, 45a, 45b, 46a, 49c, 61b, 65, 68a, 72a. Archivio Fenice, Milano: 18as, 18ad, 36a, 36c, 39as, 39ad, 39b, 46, 52d, 53s, 66a. Archivio Treves, New York: 50, 64a. Biblioteca dell'Opéra di Parigi: 55a, 31a. Collezione Ketto Cattaneo, Bergamo: 10a, 42b, 49ad, 61a, 67, 68-69a, 68c, 68b, 69c, 69b, 72b, 76, 77as, 78. ENIT, Roma, 15s. Ente Autonomo del Teatro alla Scala di Milano: 48ad. Fabbri Fotoservice, Milano: copertina, 7. Foto Saporetti, Milano: 4-5, 24s, 24d, 27a, 30s, 40a, 43a, 43c, 44a, 51a, 51b, 52s, 53d, 55bs, 55bd, 56a, 57a, 63a, 65bs, 65bc, 65bd, 68c, 73b, 80. Giancarlo Costa, Milano: 14a, 14b, 21s, 21d, 22c, 22b, 25, 26bs, 26bd, 27s, 27d, 28a, 30a, 32bs, 36b, 43b, 46b, 49b, 60as, 67bs, 67bd, 75a, 79. Kunsthinstorisches Museum, Vienna: 38. Lelli e Masotti, Milano: 11a, 18b, 19a, 19b, 28b, 58a, 58b, 59, 71a, 71bs. Louvre, Parigi: 54a. Marchi e Marchi, Pesaro: 13bd, 13ad. Museo teatrale alla Scala, Milano: 15d, 35as. James Haffernan (Metropolitan Opera House): 23s, 23d. Raccolta stampe Bertarelli, Milano: 16, 54b, 55ad, 56bd, 57b, 66b. Rossini Festival Opera Pesaro: 12, 13, 20, 22a, 32a (Rino Guarino), 62a, 62b, 63bs, 70as, 70bs, 70a, 71bd, 73a, 74a, 74b, 75b, 75c, 77d, 77b. Salzburger Marionettentheater: 32bd, 33a, 33b. Staatsbibliothek Preussischer Kulturbesitz, Berlino: 60ad.